WILD SWAZILAND

Common Animals and Plants

R Boycott   B Forrester   L Loffler   A Monadjem

Contents

INTRODUCTION AND HISTORICAL PERSPECTIVE

In Swaziland the past and the present are more strongly linked than anywhere else in Africa. Every year thousands of warriors in skins and feathered headdresses dance to sacred rhythms in ceremonies that are hundreds or thousands of years old - but the links with the past lie much deeper than this, extending far back into our early human origins.

Stone tools made over a million years ago lie on many riverbanks and show that human evolution occurred in Swaziland in a continuous sequence from our earliest ape-like origins to the present. During this period people first started mining and the worlds oldest mine, carbon dated to about 42 000 years ago, is dramatically perched on the mountain slopes of Malolotja Nature Reserve. They mined red ochre and specularite. Ochre is a very pure form of red rusted iron that was probably used for medicine, painting and body decoration. Specularite is a glittering form of crystalline iron almost certainly used for body decoration.

During this period the population of Swaziland was low, probably at the most a few thousand people who would have moved with the seasons, following the ancient rhythms of animal migrations where tens of thousands of wildebeest moved in single herds and the plains were filled with zebra and antelope of every variety.

BUSHMAN PAINTING AT NSANGWINI SHOWING EARLY BLACK SETTLERS WITH A COW AND FAT-TAILED SHEEP

The people in the last twenty thousand years or so were the direct ancestors of the Bushmen or San of today and Bushman legends and art are a direct continuation of the ancient traditions. They divided people and animals in ways that we do not - to them we were all animals: but some animals ate cooked food and others did not. They believed that in trance people could transform into animals and back again, that our bodies were not locked into one permanent shape.

They believed that there were two worlds: the world that we see and a more powerful spirit world that ultimately determines cause and effect in this world. Shamans were people uniquely gifted to be able to move between the two worlds, and to alter the balance of power. Therefore when there was stress, illness or drought the shaman would enter the spirit world, find out what was causing the problem and fix it. Bushman paintings are probably records of these voyages that shamans made into the other world, a record painted to show the group that remained behind what had happened, and why.

In about 400 AD this truly ancient and timeless hunter-gatherer lifestyle began to change when the first wave of black settlers entered the country. They came from central Africa in a slow migration down the continent, they were the early Bantu speaking peoples. The precise language that they spoke is not known. They brought a new way of life, agriculture and a new technology, iron smelting. Probably they had cattle, sheep and goats, and their staple grain was sorghum. They believed that there were two worlds; this world and the world of the ancestors, a single distant and remote creator god had brought everything into existence.

The ancestral world was the important one and it was there that all critical decisions were made. The ancestors' world mirrored the social structures of the agriculturalists who lived in

YOUNG WARRIORS MARCHING DURING THE TRADITIONAL INCWALA CEREMONY

small semi-mobile clans with clear identities and sharply defined loyalties. The ancestors had the direct interests of their living descendants at heart and could see into the future. People could hear the ancestors in dreams, or they could use a person skilled in moving between the worlds. The traditional healer, or sangoma, was able to interpret the wishes of the ancestors by communicating with them in trance.

The Bushmen were believed to be uniquely gifted in attracting rain in severe droughts, a skill that the agriculturalists lacked at that time. Rock art shelters like Nsangwini in northern Swaziland depict rainmaking rituals and there is a rare painting showing black pastoralists with their domestic animals, possibly black settlers asking for rainmaking ceremonies.

The meeting of the two groups was not always peaceful. The Bushman had difficulty in understanding how someone could 'own' an animal, to them it was like owning a bird in a tree

A TRADITIONAL HEALER, OR SANGOMA, IN FULL REGALIA

or water in a river. However the black agriculturalists definitely believed that they owned the cattle, sheep and goats that they raised and protected – and inevitably there was conflict.

In about 1200 there was a second wave of black settlers, thought to have been Sotho speakers, which increased competition for land and resources. The Bushmen were almost certainly driven from the fertile middleveld, which was attractive to agriculturalists, and sought refuge in the cold, wet, infertile highveld mountains with poor grazing in the west. There they were safe, but they were increasingly marginalized and year by year their numbers slowly declined.

In about 1500 the Dlamini clan, who were part of the Nguni peoples, lived on the southern edge of Maputo Bay, probably as vassals to the dominant Tembe clan. The bay was initially a convenient area with fresh water and fertile soil for people migrating down the coast, where after the 1540s the Portuguese established a tiny settlement. They had little interest in the southern African hinterland, as the lure of gold, silk and spices in the East was so strong that their African outposts were primarily refueling stations. Intermittent trade developed between the Tembe and the Portuguese, in which gold and ivory were exported and beads and cloth imported. Coastal access became valuable and there was competition for space on the shores of the bay. The Dlamini and a few allies left the bay and continued their migration southwards down the flat coastal plains, taking cattle, seeds and sacred power rituals that needed sea water.

The Pongola river valley offered ideal conditions for cattle grazing and agriculture in fertile soils on the silt-rich riverbanks. By 1750 the Dlamini were moving into what is now southern

Swaziland, where there were skirmishes with clans like the Ndwandwe which were already in the region, but no serious warfare. There was enough food and endless amounts of land, so there was not sufficient stress for deadly conflicts.

This situation might have continued indefinitely; however, a plant introduced by the Portuguese around 1750 was to change the whole course of history in the sub-region. The plant was maize. It was up to nine times as productive as sorghum and maize cultivation quickly spread. The population boomed. However there was a drawback to maize cultivation: it was far more drought-sensitive than sorghum. Between 1805-7 the inevitable happened - there was a severe drought and the maize crop that the increased population relied on totally failed. As the drought continued year after year, people ate their planting stock and then their cattle. There was immense social disruption and people moved from one clan to another desperately searching for food and survival. In this chaos a strong military leader emerged, Shaka, king of the Zulu. He was a negative military genius - like Hitler and Stalin, he arose out of pre-existing social chaos.

Shaka changed the nature of southern African warfare. Before him, wars were almost ritual cattle raids. There was a sound reason for this: people viewed neighboring clans as a cattle-raising asset that could be periodically exploited. If one killed them then there would be no one to raise the next generation of cattle to be raided. So war tended to be a ritual contest where each side hurled fearsome insults and a few spears at one another - and then went home. Both sides could claim victory and injures were unlikely to be widespread. Shaka changed this totally; a child of a desperate age, he attacked to kill, to annihilate and to grab territory. The new tactics needed new weapons and he invented the short stabbing spear for hand-to-hand combat to the death. Ritual fighting lay in the past. This was the start of nation formation in southern Africa as clans grouped together under military leaders for protection. Zulu expansion affected many neighbouring clans, including the Dlamini.

Under the very real threat of annihilation by the Zulus the Dlamini united the surrounding clans under themselves and effectively became kings in the 1820s and 30s. They too started conquering for its own sake, making a simple ultimatum: accept our authority and protection or 'you will sweep the ashes'. Land controlled by the Swazis expanded greatly for twenty to thirty years, far beyond its current boundaries.

During the 1800s there were increasing numbers of white settlers throughout southern Africa. The Boers wanted farmland to lead lives of self-sufficient, rigid Calvinist austerity, the British wanted minerals, particularly gold. Both groups would readily attempt to eradicate anyone who stood between them and their goals, using religious or moral justifications to do so. The white settlers had a common belief that there were two worlds - the one that we live in and a world of perpetual life after death which was spent in either heaven or hell. They also believed that they had a divine right to spread what they called the three C's - Commerce, Christianity and Civilisation. Prospectors fuelled by rot-gut gin scoured South Africa searching for minerals, dreaming of

ZEBRA AND BLESBOK IN MALOLOTJA NATURE RESERVE

instant vast wealth and using the three C's for justification - if they were ever questioned.

In the 1880s there were gold rushes in Barberton in South Africa, not far from Swaziland, and prospectors looked for gold in the sparsely populated mountainous blue-gray Swaziland highveld. In 1883/4 gold was found at Forbes Reef and Piggs Peak. The king of the Swazis at the time, Mbandzeni, was caught in a dilemma - he was squeezed between the Portuguese, the British and the Boers. The neighbouring Zulu and Pedi kingdoms had fought the colonialists, but they lost the battles, their land and their power. This was just before the colonialists arrived in Swaziland in substantial numbers. King Mbandzeni saw the results of resisting colonialism and made a compromise that he lived to regret - leasing land and concessions to the white settlers in order to preserve the throne and the nation. In retrospect this was the best decision in extremely difficult circumstances. However a totally dishonest colonist employed by the king to regulate concessions made the situation much worse until the Swazi Nation was left with no land whatsoever.

The Boers wanted Swaziland for a rail route from the rich goldfields in Johannesburg to the sea at Kosi Bay. They never formally invaded the country, but instead bought up concessions useful for running a country and clearly intended quietly absorbing Swaziland into the Transvaal Republic. The British finally agreed to the Transvaal 'administering' Swaziland in 1894 and the Boers appointed a commissioner, in effect a governor. They were able to do this because the Boers and the British had made a typically colonial deal: the Boers could 'have' Swaziland provided that the British in turn were left alone to develop Rhodesia, now Zimbabwe. However, Boer ambitions were wrecked by the second Boer War fought against the British, a war which the Boers lost in 1902. Afterwards Swaziland was unenthusiastically incorporated into the British Empire as an ill-defined protectorate that had previously been Boer 'territory'.

The British practiced indirect rule when they could - it was cheaper, easier and allowed them to take the high moral road. Two rulers, the Queen Mother Gwamile and her grandson King Sobhuza II, were basically given internal self-rule of the Swazi Nation for eighty years – so in effect, King Mbandzeni's compromise ultimately preserved Swazi independence. Although the British officially called Sobhuza the Paramount Chief, they had no objections to him holding the traditional ceremony of kingship, the Incwala. During this period, with royal support, Christianity spread widely in the form of Zionism, a blend of traditional ancestor veneration, Christian and Old Testament beliefs. To the Swazis the two world structures and single god of the Christian missionaries made perfect sense: it was merely filling in details in a pre-existing conceptual framework that they were totally familiar with. The Old Testament promoted spirit possession, speaking in tongues, prophesy, divination, sacrifices and polygamy.

Whilst there was a fairly smooth religious integration under early British colonialism, the land issue remained a serious problem and source of conflict. The British tried to sort out the chaotic concession era when land and concessions had often been ceded to several people simultaneously. In 1907 the country was formally surveyed and divided into thirds, one third going to white set-

MAJOR MILLER AND SON HUNTING IN THE 1920S OR 30S

tler farmers, one third going to the Swazi Nation and one third became British Crown Land. The Nation was totally dismayed with this and spent the next fifty years raising money to buy back more land, using money from mine workers in Johannesburg, whilst the British periodically sold Crown Land to fund their administration.

The British practiced social segregation, but it was never formalized into a brutal code like apartheid with pass laws, forced removals, beatings and imprisonment. Instead the different groups led their own lives as best they could on their various land holdings.

Most colonialists became farmers, seeing wild animals as vermin for two reasons - they ate the grass that was the basis for cattle farming and they were seen as a reservoir of disease. The British encouraged hunting in every form, even machine gunning vast herds of wildebeest. The endless herds that had once taken days to pass by died out and were replaced by barbed wire, cattle ranches, dip tanks and government stock inspectors. By the early 1960s there were few populations of wild animals left in the country and early conservation efforts met with official indifference or hostility.

The 1960s saw sweeping political changes throughout Africa and Swaziland peacefully became independent in 1968. This brought not just political change, but also changes in land use. King Sobhuza actively promoted both private and government conservation efforts, as ultimately nature reserves were the only reliable source of the rare plants and animals crucial for the ancient power rituals of kingship.

From the mid-sixties onwards the number of protected areas increased, as did the land holdings of the Swazi Nation. Today foreign-owned land is a fraction of the national total and all Swazi citizens have the right to swear allegiance to a chief, in return receiving land with communal grazing for living and farming. Communal ownership of cattle grazing land has led to extreme overgrazing - no individual has an incentive to control their cattle grazing. As a result the existing nature reserves are increasingly isolated pockets (or living museums) in the face of an incredible population increase from a mere 84 000 in 1904 to around a million today.

The reserves preserve a habitat and way of life that is more than purely ecological - it is bound up in the myth and symbolism of the monarchy where the king is the Lion and the Queen Mother the Great She Elephant. Plants and animals are widely used in traditional medicine as well as sacred rituals of power and kingship.

These are links to the past, just as during the Incwala young men walk to the ocean to fetch sea water in memory of a time hundreds of years ago when the nucleus of the Swazi nation was on the coast, the ancestors were beneath the sea and nature was boundless.

THE KOMATI AT NSANGWINI

GEOLOGY AND CROSS-SECTIONS

Swaziland's geology is a miniature of the region. In a small area there is a dramatic and very scenic transition from the high African plateau to classic African bushveld; in addition there is the geologically unique Swaziland Supergroup, also known as the Barberton Supergroup.

This area, which is in the north-west of the country and neighbouring South Africa, is heavily folded and has mineral deposits of iron, gold and asbestos. Gneiss found in the area is considered to be part of the oldest remaining crust of the planet, dating back to 3.5 billion years ago, a mere billion years after the Earth's formation. Finely grained chert within the Supergroup has fossil remains of single celled life forms within the Onverwacht, dated to 3.3 to 3.4 billion years old, perhaps relics of the first life on our planet. Lying above these are the Fig-Tree and Moodies groups which contain quartzites, shales, cherts and banded ironstone. Ancient pre-Cambrian gneiss underlies many rock formations and is the basement rock for much of the country.

The boundary between the Swaziland Supergroup and the granite regions of the country can be seen on the road from Motshane to Pigg's Peak. If one is driving through the Hawane / Forbes Reef area the western side has the soft rounded mountain tops of the Supergroup. The eastern side is granite, giving Swaziland it's characteristic 'koppie' formations - piles of granite boulders on hilltops and long curving granite ridges known as whalebacks.

Schematic cross sections of Swaziland

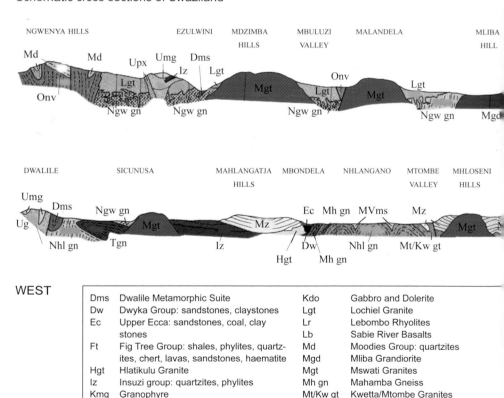

Dms	Dwalile Metamorphic Suite	Kdo	Gabbro and Dolerite
Dw	Dwyka Group: sandstones, claystones	Lgt	Lochiel Granite
Ec	Upper Ecca: sandstones, coal, clay stones	Lr	Lebombo Rhyolites
		Lb	Sabie River Basalts
Ft	Fig Tree Group: shales, phylites, quartzites, chert, lavas, sandstones, haematite	Md	Moodies Group: quartzites
		Mgd	Mliba Grandiorite
Hgt	Hlatikulu Granite	Mgt	Mswati Granites
Iz	Insuzi group: quartzites, phylites	Mh gn	Mahamba Gneiss
Kmg	Granophyre	Mt/Kw gt	Kwetta/Mtombe Granites

The sections are approximately 98 kilometres from west to east

The granite areas of the country extend through the eastern sections of the highveld well into the middleveld and lowveld in places. Batholiths of granite are quite common in the highveld – these are large rounded granite domes that originally formed deep beneath the surface and have subsequently been exposed by erosion. Their size varies, from a few hundred metres to ten kilometres or so in the case of Sibebe Rock, reputedly the world's largest batholith. The highveld escarpment forms the edge of the central African plateau, a vast flat surface extending from just beyond Swaziland's western boundary all the way to Namibia. These high flatlands are the original plateau surface of southern Africa.

The soaring mountains and deep valleys in Swaziland are the result of erosion by rivers flowing to the sea, not volcanic action or glaciation. The escarpment that they have caused extends deep into Mpumalanga to the north and as far as the kwaZulu-Natal Drakensburg in the south, geologically this whole escarpment is a single feature. It is gradually eroding westward into the high central African plateau - the flat landscape of the lowveld was eroded down from the plateau, this area of sedimentary and volcanic rocks form part of the Karoo Supergroup and were formed between the Permian and Jurassic periods. The eastern boundary of Swaziland lies on the Lebombo mountains, these were formed some 180 million years ago when basalts and rhyolites filled rifts in the original continent of Gondwanaland just before it started to break up. Over time the surrounding basalt eroded away, leaving what was once a rhyolite filled rift as blue gray mountains towering over the lowveld.

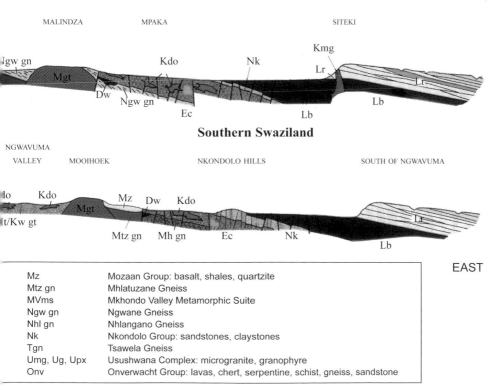

Mz	Mozaan Group: basalt, shales, quartzite	
Mtz gn	Mhlatuzane Gneiss	
MVms	Mkhondo Valley Metamorphic Suite	
Ngw gn	Ngwane Gneiss	
Nhl gn	Nhlangano Gneiss	
Nk	Nkondolo Group: sandstones, claystones	
Tgn	Tsawela Gneiss	
Umg, Ug, Upx	Usushwana Complex: microgranite, granophyre	
Onv	Onverwacht Group: lavas, chert, serpentine, schist, gneiss, sandstone	

EAST

Cross-sections courtesy of the Geological Survey and Mines Department.
From 1:250 000 Geological Map of Swaziland by Dr AC Wilson, 1982

VEGETATION TYPES AND HABITATS

Swaziland lies across the escarpment where the high central African plateau gives way to the coastal plains. As a result there is a wide range of topography and climate, this in turn has allowed a wide range of flora and fauna to flourish. The eastern region of Swaziland forms part of the Maputaland Centre of Plant Diversity (one of the world's hotspots of floral and faunal species richness and endemism), while the western region falls within two areas of global significance: the Drakensberg Escarpment Endemic Bird Area and the Barberton Centre of Plant Endemism.

Six major habitats are dominant in Swaziland; montane grassland, sour bushveld, lowveld bushveld, Lebombo bushveld, forest and wetland. These are represented in four distinct ecosystems; grassland, savanna, forest and aquatic.

GRASSLAND ECOSYSTEM

The grassland ecosystem occurs in the west of Swaziland, generally at elevations above 900 m. A dominant feature is its treeless nature, this is determined by climate and fire. Numerous woody species, however, do occur in fire-excluded areas such as rock outcrops. It is the richest ecosystem for plant species and the second richest for vertebrate species.

Montane grassland

Several grassland types in Swaziland have been grouped together for ease of reference. Included are Kangwane and Barberton montane grasslands.

Montane grassland is typified by fairly dense, short, sour to very sour grassland in rugged

MONTANE GRASSLAND

Swaziland Vegetation Map with waterbodies, major rivers and natural forests.

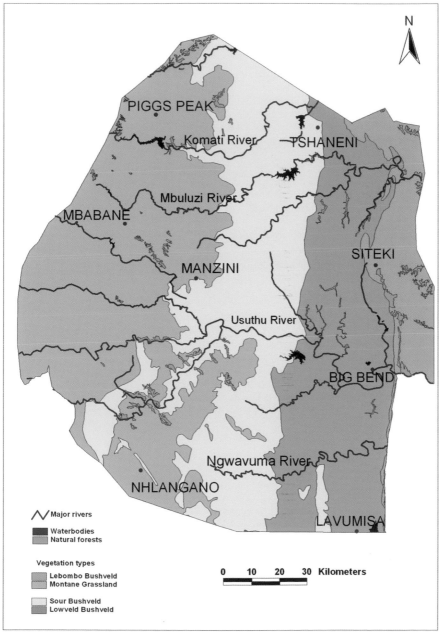

Modified from Dobson & Lotter (2004)

terrain with patches of evergreen forest occurring in ravines and river valleys. Typical grass species include *Themeda triandra, Hyparrhenia hirta, Diheteropogon amplectans, Monocymbium ceresiiforme* and *Loudetia simplex*. A large variety of shrubs and herbs also occur. Characteristic trees and shrubs which often occur in woody clumps at rock outcrops are *Englerophytum magalismontanum, Syzygium cordatum, Vangueria infausta, Cussonia* spp. and *Maesa lanceolata*.

A number of animals are restricted to these grasslands. One fish and several amphibians are restricted to wetlands in this ecosystem while a variety of reptiles, birds and some mammals, mostly small mammals but also a few larger mammals, are restricted to terrestrial habitats. These include the chubbyhead barb, raucous toad, striped stream frog, long-toed running frog, rinkhals, Swazi rock snake, common slug eater, montane speckled skink, Drakensberg crag lizard, blue swallow, Cape longclaw, long-tailed widowbird, Denham's bustard, least shrew, climbing mouse, oribi and grey rhebok.

Fire plays an important role in grasslands, changes in the fire regime can dramatically alter the vegetation which in turn affects the fauna. Grasslands burnt frequently rapidly decline in species richness. This is compounded by overgrazing which also reduces species richness, these factors explain much of the variation in habitat quality in montane grassland. Geology and soil type also influence habitat structure, for example grasslands in rocky outcrops provide suitable conditions for many plants (*Leucospermum gerrardii* and *Protea parvula*) and animals (ground woodpecker and buff-streaked chat) not found elsewhere.

Expansive stands of exotic *Acacia* spp. (wattle) smother many river and stream banks and infestations of the weeds *Solanum mauritianum* (bugweed) and *Lantana camara* (lantana) are common in disturbed areas including industrial timber plantations of *Pinus* spp. (conifer) and *Eucalyptus* spp. (gum). Much of the remaining land is settled by subsistence farmers.

SAVANNA ECOSYSTEM

The savanna ecosystem (bushveld) is the most extensive in southern Africa. It is characterised by the co-existence of grasses and trees. The density of tree and shrub cover varies widely - from a few scattered trees to 75% canopy cover including open and closed woodland and thicket. The savanna ecosystem occurs in the central, eastern and northern parts of Swaziland covering a range of altitudes between 200 - 900 m. The highest altitudes are in the west (adjacent to the grassland ecosystem) dropping gradually to the lowest altitudes in the east, but rising again in the eastern Lebombo Mountains. The specific type of savanna vegetation present at a site depends on geography, soils, impact of herbivores and fire, as well as human impact. The savanna ecosystem is very rich in species, supporting a similar number of plant species to the grassland ecosystem, but almost double the number of vertebrate species.

Sour bushveld

Several vegetation types have been combined to make up this category. Included are mixed bushveld, quartzite sourveld, Zululand sourveld and granite lowveld bushveld.

Sour bushveld generally occurs at altitudes between 400 - 900 m and the vegetation is characterised by tall grassveld with scattered trees. Some dense forest and thicket patches are often associated with rocky outcrops. Sour bushveld is generally located on steep slopes or rolling hills flattening out to the east. Typical grasses include *Hyparrhenia hirta, Hyperthelia dissoluta, Heteropogon contortus, Cymbopogon excavatus, Panicum maximum* and *Themeda triandra*. Typical trees and shrubs include *Acacia* spp., *Dombeya rotundifolia, Peltophorum africanum, Sclerocarya birrea, Gymnosporia buxifolia, Dichrostachys cinerea, Rhus* spp., *Pterocarpus angolensis, Lannea discolor, Annona senegalensis, Combretum* spp., *Euclea* spp. and *Bauhinia galpinii*.

Sour bushveld is an intergrading zone between the western temperate and the eastern subtropical regions of Swaziland and although it does support a mixed fauna there are no animals that are specifically restricted to this region. The western limits of some subtropical species reach this region, as do the eastern limits of some temperate species.

Sourveld bushveld is the most heavily settled vegetation type, the increase in population pressure is destroying natural vegetation as land is continually cleared for agricultural, rural and urban developments. Savanna may be altered rapidly by changes in fire regime, both the frequency and intensity of fire are important factors. Fire intensity is affected by overgrazing - the elimination of hot, high intensity fires results in the increased survival of saplings. This encourages bush encroachment, which in turn is often associated with a decrease in species richness. The indigenous climber *Acacia ataxacantha* and exotic *Caesalpinia decapetala* have become problem plants and tend to form impenetrable thickets along riverine fringes and in wooded areas. The invasive *Psidium guajava* continues to increase, especially around the hills of Ezulwini, Manzini and Malkerns and the indigenous *Dichrostachys cinerea* has transformed the inherent savanna around Mafutseni into thickets and dense bush.

SOUR BUSHVELD

Lowveld bushveld

For ease of reference several vegetation types have been combined to make up this category. Included are basalt sweet arid lowveld, Zululand lowveld and Delagoa lowveld.

Lowveld bushveld generally occurs at altitudes between 200 - 400 m and is split into western and eastern lowveld bushveld. The western lowveld is typically broadleaved woodland on sandy soils characterised by *Combretum* spp. and *Terminalia sericea* on steep to gentle slopes. Typical trees and shrubs are similar to the higher altitude savannas but also include *Ficus sycomorus, Peltophorum africanum, Acacia* spp., *Albizia versicolor, Grewia* spp., *Gymnosporia senegalensis, Ziziphus mucronata, Trichilia emetica* and *Lonchocarpus capassa*. Typical grasses include *Themeda triandra, Panicum maximum, Eragrostis* spp., *Eustachys paspaloides* and *Digitaria* spp.

The eastern lowveld occurs at the lowest altitudes supporting *Acacia* woodland on the flatter basaltic plains. *Acacia nigrescens* dominates in the northern parts, while drier acacia woodlands dominate the south-eastern areas of the country where rainfall is scarcer. These woodlands are *Acacia* rich including the indigenous *A. tortilis, A. borleae, A. senegal* and *A. burkei*. Open rocky outcrops covered with extensive stands of naturally occurring *Aloe marlothii* become increasingly common in this area. Other typical trees and shrubs include *Ziziphus mucronata, Sclerocarya birrea, Spirostachys africana, Gymnosporia* spp., *Dichrostachys cinerea, Euclea* spp., *Ozoroa engleri, Grewia* spp., *Bolusanthus speciosus, Combretum imberbe* and *Balanites maughamii*. Typical grasses include *Panicum maximum, Themeda triandra, Cenchrus ciliaris, Digitaria eriantha, Eragrostis spp.* and *Urochloa mossambicensis.*

The lowveld bushveld is where most of the larger mammal populations occur including elephant, rhinoceros, giraffe, zebra, wildebeest and various antelope. Bird life is prolific and a wide variety of birds of prey breed exclusively in this region such as lappet-faced vulture, bateleur, martial eagle and African hawk-eagle. The smaller vertebrates are also well represented, and this region provides suitable habitat for the highest fish, amphibian and reptile diversity in Swaziland. A few species are restricted to this region such as the tigerfish, silver catfish and ornate burrowing frog.

Overgrazing and poor fire management has resulted in bush encroachment over large areas of Nation Land, and a markedly lower diversity of birds and plants. Encroaching thicket structures dominated by the native species *Acacia nilotica* and *Dichrostachys cinerea* are common in the lowveld. Alien plant invasion is a problem especially along water courses and *Chromolaena odorata, Lantana camara, Melia azerdarach* and *Psidium guajava* have spread over large areas, while the herb *Parthenium hysterophorus* is evident in the grass layer in disturbed areas.

LOWVELD BUSHVELD

Lebombo bushveld

The steep escarpment of the Lebombo range rises from the flat lowveld at around 200 m up to 800 m and is dissected with steep gorges supporting patches of drier scarp and *Androstachys* forest. The escarpment supports a *Combretum* rich bushveld thinning out to a tall grassy plateau surrounded by rocky outcrops and cliff faces. Bush clumps around rocky outcrops are frequent on the plateau with seasonal pans occasionally forming in natural depressions. Characteristic trees and shrubs include *Combretum* spp., *Olea europaea, Berchemia zeyheri, Heteropyxis natalensis* and *Diospyros dicrophylla.*

The Lebombo bushveld supports a similar community of subtropical forms to that of the lowveld bushveld. Generally fewer mammal species are present and these occur at lower densities. Common species include grey duiker, impala, kudu and nyala. The area boasts a diverse amphibian, reptile and bird fauna. A number of endemic or near-endemic reptile species, such as the Natal hinged tortoise, occur in the region. Common birds include chinspot batis, black cuckooshrike, white-browed scrub-robin and white-bellied sunbird.

This range is important for conserving several threatened plants (e.g. some cycads and aloes) that are restricted to the rhyolitic rocks of the Lebombos.

FOREST ECOSYSTEM

This ecosystem is highly restricted and is characterised by woody plants with a continuous canopy where evergreen trees dominate. In Swaziland forest vegetation is usually found at moderate to high elevations, mainly in the west and in ravines of the Lebombo Mountains. At high altitudes forest patches are interspersed amongst the grassland and play an important role in supporting biodiversity. Forests are legendary for high species diversity, however they are easily degraded by humans. Increased exploitation, high grazing pressure, livestock trampling, pathways, veld fires and slash and burn clearing all threaten the natural vegetation. Over-harvesting of woody plants quickly opens up and dries forests exposing them to fire. Although periodic fires are a natural and necessary component of grasslands and savannas, they have a devastating effect on forests.

Swaziland's forests can be divided into three broad categories: Afromontane forests (mostly at altitudes above 1 000 m), riverine forests (mostly at altitudes below 800 m) and moist and dry forests in the Lebombo Mountains.

Generally with the exception of birds, some amphibians and some reptiles, vertebrates are poorly represented in forest habitats. Invertebrates are well represented by butterflies, moths, spiders and scorpions.

Afromontane forest

Small pockets of species-rich Afromontane forest are found along the mountain ranges predominantly in the west of the country, many of which lie above the mist belt line (e.g. Mgwayisa forest in northern Malolotja Nature Reserve and Devil's Bridge forest near Bulembu). Typical plant species include *Englerophytum magalismontanum, Syzygium cordatum, Syzygium gerrardii, Psychotria capensis, Diospyros whyteana, Maesa lanceolata, Cussonia spp., Gymnosporia harveyana, Heteropyxis spp., Peddiea africana, Scolopia spp., Trichocladus grandiflorus, Ficus spp., Dalbergia armata, Xymalos monospora, Combretum kraussi, Clausena anisata,* and *Rhus spp.*

With the exception of birds and some amphibians, vertebrates are not well represented in Afromontane forest. However, some frogs such as the Natal ghost frog and plaintive rain frog, and several bird species such as the bush blackcap, olive bush-shrike, brown scrub-robin, orange ground-thrush and Knysna turaco are restricted to this habitat.

Riverine forest

Riverine forest is associated with the major rivers. They generally occur below 800 m, and support a tall forest or closed woodland structure, often infringed by thicket. Characteristic trees along river margins include *Ficus sycomorus, Trichilia emetica, Syzygium cordatum, Breonadia salicina, Acacia robusta* and *Bridelia micrantha*. Major threats include harvesting of timber for construction, invasion by exotic plants and bush clearing for agriculture. Flooding has transformed many of these riparian zones, removing large trees from the river banks and exposing previously wooded areas. Alien invasive plants can be prolific along the low-lying riverbanks, especially the more aggressive weeds, *Chromolaena odorata, Lantana camara* and *Melia azedarach*.

With the exception of birds and some reptiles, vertebrates are poorly represented in riverine forests. Typical animals include arboreal snakes and lizards such as vine snake, boomslang, Cape dwarf gecko and southern tree agama, as well as thicket-loving birds and mammals such as pink-throated twinspot, gorgeous bush-shrike, eastern nicator, red duiker and bushbuck.

Lebombo forest

The forests of the Lebombo Mountains are generally found in ravines and along drainage lines in the extreme eastern part of the country and support a rich and varied biodiversity. Most of these forests are dry but the south-facing valleys provide shelter to several moister patches. Conspicuous stands of *Androstachys johnsonii* (Lebombo ironwood) are often found within the drier forest types harbouring interesting succulents such as *Haworthia limifolia* and *Gasteria batesiana*. The tall *Erythrophleum lasianthum* tree often forms part of the forest canopy, with typical species such as *Teclea gerrardii, Drypetes arguta, Acalypha glabrata, Chionanthus foveolatus* and *Justicia campylostemon* making up much of the understorey. A number of rare or range-restricted species occur within the forests such as the cycads *Encephalartos umbeluziensis* and *E. aplanatus*. Infestation by alien invasive species is becoming one of the more serious threats especially that of *Chromolaena odorata, Lantana camara* and *Melia azedarach*.

With the exception of birds, vertebrates are poorly represented in Lebombo forest. Typical animals occurring in this habitat include African barred owlet, African broadbill and samango monkey.

LOWVELD RIVERINE FOREST

AQUATIC ECOSYSTEM (WETLAND)

The aquatic ecosystem comprises both natural and man-made wetlands. A wide variety of aquatic habitats is represented in Swaziland consisting of rivers, streams, marshes and seasonally inundated wetlands such as pans. Borrow-pits or shallow quarries adjacent to roads that become flooded during the rainy season are important wetland habitats for amphibians and some waterbirds. Several dams have been constructed on the larger rivers and these support important populations of fish, amphibians, reptiles, many waterbirds and some mammals.

The aquatic ecosystem supports a rich biodiversity and plays an important role in the functioning of other ecosystems. No endemic species occur in this ecosystem and few aquatic plants are currently threatened. However, a significant number of aquatic vertebrates are under threat. These include numerous species of fishes, amphibians and waterbirds whose habitats have become increasingly degraded or destroyed. Alien plant invasion along river valleys is a problem, especially from *Acacia mearnsii, Sesbania punicea, Caesalpinia decapetala, Chromolaena odorata, Lantana camara* and in places the aquatic weed, *Salvinia molesta.*

Certain habitats in the aquatic ecosystem are extremely fragile. For example, the high altitude marshes and vlei systems, generally found above 1 000 m, are easily degraded and destroyed by cattle grazing, fire and cultivation. Small, but often deep, ancient seasonal pans on the Lebombo plateau support unique aquatic plants such as *Nymphoides indica* and the *Marsilea* fern.

Typical animals include numerous fishes and amphibians, terrapins and crocodiles, a variety of duck, herons and other waterbirds, as well as small and large mammals such as the water mongoose, Cape clawless otter and hippopotamus. With regard to fishes, species diversity increases towards the lower reaches of Swaziland's rivers in the north and east of the country. Similarly, amphibian species diversity is high in the subtropical bushveld regions and more than twenty species may be found breeding at some lowveld sites, particularly at seasonal pans. While the majority of fish and amphibian species occur in the north-eastern and eastern subtropical regions there are some that are restricted to the western temperate regions of the country.

WETLAND

Mammals

For many people large mammals like elephant, rhino and lion are closely associated with African landscapes and the continent is indeed rich in large mammals - but its small mammalian diversity is just as impressive. A total of 131 species of mammals has been recorded from Swaziland of which 43 species are rodents, shrews and bats.

For much of the last century, Swaziland's large mammal populations suffered at the hands of hunters and poachers. All species declined dramatically, many to extinction. By 1960 the only viable populations of antelope left in Swaziland were confined to what is now Hlane Royal National Park. Thanks to the foresight of King Sobhuza II, Hlane became a protected area and seeded populations of antelope in other parts of the country. Despite some significant success stories, many threats to mammals still exist and currently 30 species are facing extinction. Large mammals once roamed widely throughout the country and the older generation remember prolific game in the eastern lowveld. However these species are now confined to protected areas and are best viewed in the nation's parks and nature reserves.

Although abundant, most small mammals are difficult to locate or observe. However, some species of bat, such as free-tailed bats, regularly roost in roofs of houses and can be observed departing their roosts at traditional exit holes. Other species, such as horseshoe bats, roost in large numbers in certain caves and abandoned mines and can be readily approached.

All larger mammal species known to occur in Swaziland are listed here. However, many species of bats and rodents cannot be positively identified without laboratory examination. There are a few exceptions and these are presented here. For further reading, recommended books include Stuart & Stuart (1992), Skinner & Chimimba (2005) and Taylor (2000). Monadjem (1998) presents distribution maps and natural history notes for all the mammals occurring in the country, while Monadjem et al. (2003) reviews the conservation status of these species.

Forest shrew

Myosorex varius, Ingoto

Occurs in the montane grassland region, where it is associated with dense grassy areas. Rare or absent from over-grazed areas, or sites which are burnt annually. Shrews are difficult to tell apart in the field. Identified by **lack of long bristles on tail.** Fur is uniform greyish-black. Differs from the dark-footed forest shrew *M. cafer* by **pale hind feet** and **unicoloured** tail. Feeds on insects and worms. Breeds in summer months.

Mass: 11 g

Giant musk shrew

Crocidura flavescens, Ingoto

Occurs throughout the montane grassland region. Associated with dense grassland and the forest/grassland ecotone. Difficult to distinguish from other species of *Crocidura*, but is generally **larger.** The lesser red musk shrew *C. hirta* is slightly smaller and widespread in bushveld regions. **Long tail bristles** distinguish all members of this genus from genus *Myosorex* (above). Fur is reddish-brown. It is aggressive and bites readily.

Mass 22 g

Hottentot golden mole
Amblysomus hottentotus, Imvukazane
Restricted to the montane grasslands. Occurs in moist habitats, including gardens in Mbabane, where it excavates extensive burrows. Identified by **dark golden-brown fur, tiny eyes and enlarged claws on forelimbs** used for burrowing. Differs from mole-rats by **lacking enlarged incisors**. Unlike the mole-rat, this species does not do any harm to gardens as it feeds entirely on insects and worms. Little is known about its biology.
Mass: 70 g

G

Wahlberg's epauletted fruit bat
Epomophorus wahlbergi, Ligobongco
Widespread in wooded habitats, but absent from the extreme west. Most abundant in riparian forest along large rivers. Identified by **large size, dog-like muzzle, large eyes and white patches at the base of the ears**. Male has white shoulder epaulettes. Indistuiguishable from Peter's epauletted fruit bat *E. gambianus* in the field. Roosts by day in tall, leafy tree. Has an extended breeding season giving birth to a single young per attempt.
Mass: 100 g

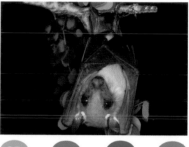

 SB   B   F   L

Little free-tailed bat
Chaerephon pumilus, Lilulwane
Widespread in the bushveld in various habitats, but often roosts in association with humans. Has a dark body, **tail which extends beyond tail membrane and wrinkled upper lip**. Smaller than the Angolan free-tailed bat *Mops condylurus* with which it often co-occurs. Roosts predominantly in roofs of houses, where it may become a nuisance. Breeds two or three times per annum, giving birth to a single young on each occasion.
Mass: 11 g

 SB   B   L

Geoffroy's horseshoe bat
Rhinolophus clivosus, Lilulwane
Occurs sparsely in montane grassland. Roosts in caves, and forages in surrounding areas. The elaborate **horse-shoe structure on the nose** is used to focus the sound signal used for echolocation (navigation by sonar). **Larger** than other horse-shoe bats in the country. Large numbers hibernate in high-altitude caves during winter. Female gives birth to a single young in early summer. Listed as "Near Threatened" in the Swazi RDB.
Mass: 16 g

G

ARA MONADJEM

G SB B

Natal long-fingered bat
Miniopterus natalensis, Lilulwane
Occurs widely but sparsely. Forages about the
canopy, but requires suitable cave for roosting
during the day. Identified by mouse-like face,
small eyes and **very long second phalanx of
third digit**. Roosts by the hundreds or thousands
in appropriate caves. Hibernates in high-altitude
caves during the winter months. Female moves
to lower altitudes to give birth to a single young.
Listed as "Near Threatened" in the Swazi RDB.
Mass: 11 g

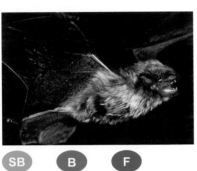

ERNEST SEAMARK

SB B F

Banana bat
Neoromicia africanus, Lilulwane
Occurs widely in bushveld. Roosts in furled banana leaves and forages in nearby riparian forest
and dense woodland. A very small bat difficult to
distinguish from other small vespers, but has distinctly **swollen pads on thumb** which are used to
cling to the inner surface of banana leaves. Each
roost occupied by a single male and one or more
females. Bats frequently change roosts as leaves
unfurl. Single young born in summer months.
Mass: 4 g

LEX HES

F

Thick-tailed bushbaby
Otolemur crassicaudatus, Singwe
Occurs throughout the country. Closely associated with well-wooded habitats where the animal is
able to move between trees without descending
to the ground. It is most abundant in riparian forest along large rivers. It is easily identified by uniform **grey-brown fur, very large eyes and long
bushy tail**. Utters a very loud penetrating wail,
most frequently heard in winter months. Urinates
on its hands, presumably to mark its territory.
Mass: 1.3 kg

PIETER DE WAAL

SB F B L

Vervet monkey
Chlorocebus aethiops, Ingobiyane
Occurs widely throughout the country, absent
only from open grasslands. Associated with
wooded habitats including forests, forest edge,
woodland and gardens. Easily identified by **greyish fur and facial markings**. The next species
is larger, darker and restricted to forest patches
in the Lebombos. The vervet monkey appears to
have declined in the past few decades, having disappeared from much of Swazi Nation Land.
Mass: 5.5 kg

Samango monkey
Cercopithecus mitis, Insimango
Restricted to forest patches in the Lebombo
Mountains. Differs from the previous species by
larger size and dark fore limbs. Diurnal and
lives in troops. Difficult to see, but located by its
booming call. Eats fruits, leaves, stems and insects. More arboreal than previous species, rarely
descending to the ground. Listed as "Endangered"
in the Swazi RDB.

Mass: 7 kg

ADAM RILEY

F

Chacma baboon
Papio hamadryas, Imfene
Widely but sparsely distributed. Mostly confined
to protected areas, but also outside these areas in
remote mountainous parts of montane grasslands
and Lebombos. Occurs in almost any habitat, but
requires either cliffs or tall trees for roosting in at
night. Troops are highly structured and complex,
with dominance hierarchies within both male and
female lines. High ranking males and females en-
joy more benefits than other troop members.
Mass: 20 kg

PHIL PERRY

G **SB** **B** **L**

Scrub hare
Lepus saxatilis, Logwaja
Occurs widely throughout the country. Associated
with open grassy habitats, especially short grasslands. Identified by **greyish-brown body and
long ears**. The Natal red hare *Pronolagus crassicaudatus* is reddish-brown in colour and restricted
to rocky outcrops. A nocturnal species that feeds
on grass, lying up under a bush during the day.
Despite heavy hunting pressure, this species still
persists on Swazi Nation Land.
Mass 1.2 kg

PHIL PERRY

G **SB** **B** **L**

Porcupine
Hystrix africaeaustralis, Ingungunbane
Occurs sparsely throughout the country. Tolerates
a wide range of habitats. Unmistakable with **long
needle-like quills on back and tail.** Feeds on
roots and tubers which it digs up. Lives in pairs
which defend a territory. A nocturnal species
which lies up in a burrow during the day. Each
territory has several burrows that the pair moves
between. Has been killed by leopard in Malolotja
Nature Reserve.
Mass: 12 kg

PHIL PERRY

G **SB** **B** **L**

SB B F L

Woodland dormouse

Graphiurus murinus, Ligundvwane

Occurs widely in the country. May inhabit a variety of habitats, often entering homes where it builds a nest in a concealed place. Easily identified by **long greyish fur, bushy tail and bold facial markings**. However, can be confused with the similar rock dormouse *G. platyops* which is less common and has a flattened skull. It is a nocturnal species that forages equally well on the ground and in bushes. Feeds on fruit and insects.

Mass: 26 g

W

Cane-rat

Thryonomys swinderianus, Livondvo

Occurs widely in suitable habitat in the bushveld regions. However, has disappeared from much of Swazi Nation Land due to over-harvesting. Closely associated with reed-beds and rank grassland near rivers and marshes, but may forage in adjacent savanna. Easily identified by **large size, uniform light brown fur, and rodent-like features**. An average of four young are born after a gestation period of five months.

Mass: 4 kg

G SB B L

Natal multimammate mouse

Mastomys natalensis, Ligundvwane

This is undoubtably the most abundant vertebrate in Swaziland. Widespread and associated with disturbed landscapes such as recently burnt veld, agricultural fields and semi-urban areas. It lacks any conspicuous features and has a **uniform greyish-brown fur**. Numbers fluctuate greatly between seasons and years, with regular eruptions after good rainfall. May give birth to up to 22 young every couple of months, but is short-lived.

Mass: 40 g

G SB

Striped mouse

Rhabdomys pumilio, Ligundvwane

Occurs widely in the west. Tolerates a wide range of habitats including grassland and cultivated fields, but requires dense grass or shrub. Has **sandy-brown fur with conspicuous black-and-white stripes** running down its back. Active during the day and often heard scurrying through the grass. One of the most abundant rodents in montane grassland. Young are born in a burrow or a grass nest concealed in dense vegetation.

Mass: 35 g

Aardwolf
Proteles cristatus, Singci
In Swaziland, restricted to open grassy areas at high altitudes. Regularly sighted only in Malolotja Nature Reserve. Has **hyena-like appearance with vertical black stripes along body**. Usually nocturnal, but seen singly or in pairs during late afternoon in winter. Feeds on termites, licking with elongated tongue. Roosts in abandoned antbear burrows where young are born. "Near Threatened" in the Swazi RDB.
Mass: 8 kg

Spotted hyaena
Crocuta crocuta, Impisi
Occurs only in Hlane National Park, Mkhaya Game Reserve and surrounding areas. Tolerates a wide range of habitats. Unmistakable with **large head, sloping body and variable spotting pattern**. In Swaziland only seen at night singly or in small family groups. Is a capable hunter, but also scavenges. Young are born in a den that may be a cave or burrow in the ground. Listed as "Vulnerable" in the Swazi RDB.
Mass: 70 kg

Cape clawless otter
Aonyx capensis, Intsini
Occurs sparsely along undisturbed rivers and streams throughout the country. Identified by **typical otter appearance**; the only otter species occurring in Swaziland. Very rarely seen, but otter signs are frequently encountered along rivers and streams, in particular the scat, consisting of crushed crab exoskeleton. Highly aquatic, swimming in search of crabs and fish. Young are born in dens near water's edge.
Mass: 14 kg

Cheetah
Acinonyx jubatus, Lihlosi
Occurs only at Hlane National Park, where a small number have been re-introduced. Unmistakable, easily distinguished from leopard by **delicate build and black "tear drops"** on face. Associated with open savanna, avoiding areas favoured by lions. Hunts small antelope up to the size of impala which it catches by high speed chase, exceeding 100 km/hr. Listed as "Regionally Extinct" in the Swazi RDB.
Mass: 50 kg

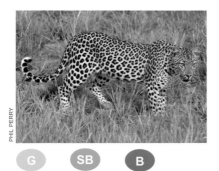

PHIL PERRY

G SB B

Leopard
Panthera pardus, Ingwe
Very sparsely distributed. Occurs at Malolotja Nature Reserve, Mlilwane Wildlife Sanctuary and Hlane National Park; a vagrant elsewhere. Wide habitat tolerance, but requires cover for hunting. Unmistakable **robust build and spotting pattern**. Feeds on medium-sized antelope, hunting by wait-and-ambush strategy. Typically drags prey up a large tree where it is safe from other predators. "Near Threatened" in the Swazi RDB.
Mass: 60 kg

PHIL PERRY

B

Lion
Panthera leo, Libhubesi
Occurs at Hlane National Park, where a small number has been re-introduced. Also present in a very small enclosure at Nisela Safaris. Unmistakable. Tolerates a wide range of habitats. Preys on a variety of antelope species, but at Hlane supplementary food is provided. Highly territorial, each pride requiring a large area, posing problems in small local reserves. Listed as "Near Threatened" in the Swazi RDB.
Mass: 150 kg

PHIL PERRY

G SB B

Serval
Leptailurus serval, Indloti
Regularly sighted only at Malolotja Nature Reserve and Mlilwane Wildlife Sanctuary, scarce elsewhere. Associated with tall, rank grassland. Easily identified by **medium size, light brown fur with black spots**. Usually seen singly, hunting for rodents which it listens for with large ears, pouncing when prey has been located. Listed as "Near Threatened" in the Swazi RDB.

Mass: 10 kg

PHIL PERRY

G SB B L

Black-backed jackal
Canis mesomelas, Inkalwane
Occurs sparsely and patchily in a wide range of habitats. Has **fox-like appearance, reddish-brown fur with black back**. The similar-sized side-striped jackal *C. adustus* has a conspicuous white tip to the tail. A nocturnal species when disturbed. More frequently heard, uttering unique wailing sounds, than seen in Swaziland. Numbers fluctuate greatly as a result of disease, particularly rabies. Rarely recorded outside of protected areas.
Mass: 8 kg

Large-spotted genet
Genetta tigrina, Insimba

Occurs widely, but scarce in the extreme western montane grasslands. Identified by **small size, greyish-brown coat with black spots and bushy tail barred with black rings**. Occurs in a wide range of wooded habitats, most abundant in savanna, but also in riparian forest, bushclump and exotic plantations. Seen singly foraging on the ground or in trees for rodents, birds and fruit. The coat is sought after for the making of loin skins.

Mass: 1.8 kg

G **SB** **B** **F** **L**

Slender mongoose
Galerella sanguineus, Imbolwane

Occurs throughout the country, reaching highest densities in sparsely populated agricultural areas. Associated with a range of habitats, but requires some form of cover, usually tall or dense grass. Identified by **rufous-brown fur and tail with a conspicuous black tip**. Tail is often held high when running away from danger. Feeds predominantly on rodents.

Mass: 0.6 kg

G **SB** **B** **L**

Dwarf mongoose
Helogale parvula, Mashigoti

Widespread in the bushveld regions. Occurs in a variety of savanna habitats, but requires dense ground cover usually in the form of tall grass. Identified by **very small size and uniform dark brown fur**. Roosts by night in burrows, often in termite or ant mounds. Lives in small groups of up to a dozen individuals. Feeds mainly on insects located by digging and scraping the soil surface. Only the alpha male and female breed.

Mass: 0.3 kg

B

Banded mongoose
Mungos mungo, Sikhekhekhe

Occurs widely but sparsely in the central and northern bushveld. Associated with wooded savanna or forest edge. Has **grey-brown fur with bold bands across the back**. Lives in packs of up to 20 that move through the undergrowth, foraging for insects. Active only during the day, sleeping in burrows especially disused termitaria. Dominant members of the pack hierarchy raise far more offspring than lower ranking individuals.

Mass: 1.3 kg

B

Antbear
Orycteropus afer, Sambane
Occurs sparsely but widely in almost any habitat, but avoids forest interior. Unmistakable, cannot be confused with any other animal. Uses its very powerful forelimbs armed with robust claws to dig burrows. Strictly nocturnal, feeding predominantly on ants and termites which it collects on its long sticky tongue. Ant mound or termitarium is broken with claw and tongue is inserted deep into the nest. Sleeps in burrows during the day.
Mass: 55 kg

African elephant
Loxodonta africana, Indlovu
Occurs in Hlane National Park and Mkhaya Game Reserve, where it was re-introduced in the 1980s. A pair from neighbouring Songimvelo Nature Reserve in South Africa has settled and successfully bred in the Komati valley within Malolotja Nature Reserve. Requires a huge amount of food and water; eating up to 80 kg of plant material and 160 l of water per day. A single calf is born after a gestation period of about 22 months.
Mass: up to 6 000 kg

Rock hyrax
Procavia capensis, Imbila
Occurs sparsely but widely throughout the montane grassland. Prefers rocky outcrops and boulder-strewn landscapes, in either open grassland or woodland. Has **dumpy rabbit-sized body, dark brown fur and pointed muzzle**. Lives colonially; a successful male defending a territory which provides shelter for his harem. Feeds on plant matter that may be grazed well away from rocks. Staple diet of Verreauxs' eagle *Aquila verreauxii.*
Mass: 3.5 kg

Squarelipped (white) rhinoceros
Ceratotherium simum, Umkhombe
Has been re-introduced to Hlane National Park and Mhkaya Game Reserve. Is **larger** than the next species with a conspicuously **square lip**. Feeds on grass, spending a considerable amount of the day grazing. Poaching caused a massive decline in the 1980s. This has since come under control and the population has steadily increased since the early 1990s. Gives birth to a single calf after a gestation period of 15 months.
Mass: 1 200 kg

Hooklipped (black) rhinoceros

Diceros bicornis, Bejane
Only present at Mkhaya Game Reserve where it has been re-introduced. Differs from the previous species by conspicuously **pointed lip**. A browser that feeds on a variety of plants, including stems which it characteristically cuts at 45° angle. This species has experienced the largest population decline and range contraction of any large mammal in Africa in the past century. The Swazi population is currently secure and on the increase.
Mass: 900 kg

Burchell's zebra

Equus burchelli, Lidvuba
Occurs in most protected areas in the country. Associated with savanna habitats, but was introduced to montane grassland in Malolotja Nature Reserve where it is thriving. Unmistakable; **horse-like** animal with **black-and-white stripes**. A grazer that feeds on a variety of coarse grasses. Lives in family groups, with a stallion defending a harem of females from other males. Males unable to defend females form bachelor herds.
Mass: 310 kg

Warthog

Phacochoerus aethiopicus, Budzayikatane
Occurs in most protected areas in the country. Also present on a number of protected cattle ranches such as IYSIS Ranch near Tshaneni. Associated with savanna habitats but has been successfully introduced to Malolotja Nature Reserve. Unmistakable. Diurnal, lying up in a burrow at night. Typical burrows have multiple entrances and may be occupied by several warthogs. It grazes and digs for roots with its tusks.
Mass: 70 kg

Bushpig

Potamochoerus porcus, Ingulube
Occurs sparsely in suitable habitat throughout much of the country, but scarce or absent where persecuted. Associated with dense woodland, riparian forest and forest edge. Readily enters cane fields where it may damage the crop. Differs from previous species by **hunched back, small tusks and "beard"**. Lives in small family groups, laying up in a thicket during the day and foraging at night.
Mass: 75 kg

PHIL PERRY

Hippopotamus
Hippopotamus amphibius, Imvubu
Occurs sparsely along the Komati, Umbuluzi and Usuthu river systems and associated dams. Closely associated with water during the day, spending most of the time either submerged, or sunning itself on a sandy bank. Unmistakable. Male defends territory against other males often escalating into fights which may result in serious injuries to one or both animals. Successful male will inherit the harem. Grazes on land at night.
Mass: 1 400 kg

W

PHIL PERRY

Giraffe
Giraffa camelopardalis, Indlulamitsi
Has been re-introduced to a number of protected areas in the country. Associated with savanna habitats. Unmistakable. Lives in loose family herds. Male may fight another male for access to female. This involves striking the opponent with a side swing of the long neck. Due to its large size it is free from the threat of most predators, but is vulnerable to lions.

Mass: 950 kg

SB **B**

PHIL PERRY

Impala
Aepyceros melampus, Imphala
The most abundant antelope in Swaziland, occurring in bushveld regions in protected areas and some cattle ranches. Associated with savanna, but was introduced to montane grasslands at Malolotja Nature Reserve where it has not fared particularly well. Identified by **reddish-brown coat fading to white belly**, and characteristic **black glands** on the back of the lower hindlegs. Culled in protected areas to prevent over-grazing.
Mass: 45 kg

SB **B** **L**

PHIL PERRY

Red hartebeest
Alcelaphus buselaphus, Ingolongwane
Occurs only at Malolotja Nature Reserve where it has been introduced. This species did not historically occur in Swaziland. It is typically associated with the arid western parts of southern Africa. Easily identified by **reddish coat and characteristically-shaped horns** which are present in both sexes. Calves at Malolotja are dropped in September and October.

Mass: 130 kg

G

Black wildebeest

Connochaetes gnou, Ingongonyane
Occurs only at Malolotja Nature Reserve where it has been introduced. It did not historically occur in Swaziland and is typically associated with the grassy plains of the South African plateau. Differs from the next species by **white tail and characteristically-shaped horns,** present in both sexes. At Malolotja tends to inhabit higher altitudes than the next species, but the possibility of hybridization between the two species is a serious concern.
Mass: 140 kg

G

Blue wildebeest

Connochaetes taurinus, Ingongoni
Occurs in most of the country's protected areas, as well as some cattle ranches. Associated with savanna habitats, but has been introduced to Malolotja Nature Reserve where it may be hybridizing with the previous species. Differs from the previous species by **dark tail and differently-shaped horns**, present in both sexes. A grazer that often forages alongside zebra. In Swaziland, calves mostly dropped in December.
Mass: 210 kg

G   SB   B

Blesbok

Damaliscus dorcus, Linoni
Occurs in a number of protected areas and private ranches in the west of the country. In former times it would only have been an irregular visitor to the extreme western parts of the country. Identified by **dark brown coat, white forehead** and characteristically-shaped **horns** which have a thicker base in the male than the female. The rut takes place between March and May, and calves are dropped in late October or early November.
Mass: 70 kg

G   SB

Tsessebe

Damaliscus lunulatus, Umzansi
Has been re-introduced to Mkhaya Game Reserve and Mhlosinga Nature Reserve. Differs from the previous species by **black forehead** and shape of the **horns**. Reputed to be the fastest antelope in southern Africa. The rut takes place in February and calves are dropped during November or December after a gestation period of 8 months. Listed as "Near Threatened" in the Swazi RDB book.
Mass: 130 kg

B

F

Red duiker
Cephalophus natalensis, Umsumphe
Occurs sparsely in suitable habitat in a few parts of the country. Closely associated with densely wooded situations, especially forest. Identified by **small size and reddish-brown coat**. The next species is larger and has a greyish-brown coat. Short straight horns are only present in the male. Usually seen singly, very occasionally in pairs. A selective browser. Listed as "Near Threatened" in the Swazi RDB book.
Mass: 14 kg

G **SB** **B** **F** **L**

Grey duiker
Sylvicapra grimmia, Impunzi
The most widespread antelope in Swaziland, but less numerous than impala. Associated with a wide range of habitats from montane grasslands to forest edge; but requires good cover in which to conceal itself. Identified by **small size and coarse greyish-brown coat**. The similar-sized steenbok has a sleek straw-coloured coat. Only the male has horns. Its coat is sought after for traditional male attire.
Mass: 19 kg

G **SB** **B** **L**

Klipspringer
Oreotragus oreotragus, Ligoga
Occurs very patchily in the country, mostly confined to protected areas. Closely associated with cliffs and boulder-strewn habitats. Identified by **coarse greyish-brown coat** and conspicuous **black orbital gland**. The only antelope that habitually frequents rocky terrain, effortlessly negotiating steep rock faces. Often seen in pairs; may leave rocky outcrop to forage. Listed as "Near Threatened" in the Swazi RDB book.
Mass: 12 kg

G **L**

Oribi
Ourebia ourebi, Liwula
Very restricted distribution in Swaziland. It once occurred throughout the montane grasslands and the Lebombo plateau. The Lebombo population is now thought to be extinct. Occurs naturally only in Malolotja Nature Reserve, but was introduced to Mkhaya Game Reserve and Mlilwane Wildlife Sanctuary. A beautiful antelope with an **orangish-brown coat with contrasting pure white belly**. "Vulnerable" in the Swazi RDB book.
Mass: 14 kg

PHIL PERRY

Grey rhebok

Pelea capreolus, Liza
Regularly sighted only in Malolotja Nature
Reserve in montane grassland. Prefers undulating
hilly country but also occurs on rocky outcrops
and ridges at altitudes above 1 000 m. Identified
by **medium size and greyish coat**. The straight
horns, present only in males, differ from mountain reedbuck. Seen singly or in small family
groups. Runs off when disturbed showing white
under-tail. "Vulnerable" in the Swazi RDB book.
Mass: 20 kg

G

Steenbok

Raphicerus campestris, Lingcina
Occurs sparsely in the bushveld; mostly confined
to protected areas and more remote cattle ranches. Associated with open *Acacia tortilis* savanna, avoiding dense woodland. Identified by **sleek
buffy-brown coat and white belly**. The oribi is
larger and has a more shaggy coat. The straight
horns are present only in the male. Almost always
seen in pairs. Like the grey duiker is able to survive
outside of protected areas.
Mass: 11 kg

B

Roan antelope

Hippotragus equinus
Occurs at Mkhaya Game Reserve where it has
been re-introduced. Has also recently been introduced to Mlilwane Game Reserve. In former
times was restricted to the far north-eastern parts
of the bushveld region, where it is now extinct.
Differs from the next species by **greyish coat and
shape of horns** which are present in both sexes.
Listed as "Near Threatened" in the Swazi RDB
book.
Mass: 270 kg

B

Sable antelope

Hippotragus niger
Occurs at Mkhaya Game Reserve where it has
been introduced.There is no evidence to suggest
that it occurred in Swaziland in historic times.
Differs from the previous species by **black coat
in the male or reddish-brown coat in the female**. Horn is uniquely-shaped and present in
both sexes. Listed as "Near Threatened" in the
Swazi RDB book.

Mass: 230 kg

B

PHIL PERRY

B

African buffalo
Syncerus caffer, Inyatsi
Has been re-introduced to Mkhaya Game Reserve, and recently to Mlilwane Game Reserve. Identified by **very large size, robust build and dark coat**. Elsewhere occurs in large migrating mixed-sex herds. Old non-breeding males form bachelor herds. Good habitat exists at Hlane National Park, but has not been re-introduced due to the threat of foot-and-mouth disease. Listed as "Near Threatened" in the Swazi RDB book.
Mass: 600 kg

PHIL PERRY

G

B

Eland
Taurotragus oryx, Imphofu
Has been re-introduced to Malolotja Nature Reserve and Mkhaya Game Reserve. The Malolotja animals have settled down well and are breeding. Easily identified by **very large size, light coat and spiral horns** present in both sexes. A grazer that exhibits altitudinal migration elsewhere in its range, forming large herds in summer breaking up to smaller groups in winter.

Mass: 500 kg

PHIL PERRY

SB

B

L

Kudu
Tragelaphus strepsiceros, Lishongololo
Occurs sparsely and patchily throughout the country, mostly in protected areas and larger cattle ranches. Associated with a variety of wooded habitats. Easily identified by **greyish coat with very large spiral horns** present only in the male. The next species has darker coat, orangish legs and smaller horns. Seen singly or in small family groups. Males do not defend territories, but establish a dominance hierarchy.
Mass: 220 kg

PHIL PERRY

SB
B

Nyala
Tragelaphus angasii, Inyala
Has been re-introduced to a number of protected areas and ranches in the country. Associated with denser habitat than the previous species. **Male** easily identified by **dark shaggy coat, orangish legs and spiral horns. Female has reddish-brown coat with conspicuous vertical white stripes**. Usually in small family groups. Grazes during the wet season, switching to browsing in the dry season.
Mass: 80 kg

Bushbuck
Tragelaphus scriptus, Imbabala
Occurs widely but patchily in suitable habitat in protected areas and remote cattle ranches. Associated with densely wooded areas. In Swaziland, highest densities probably in riparian forest in low-lying savannas. **Male** differs from previous two species by **smaller size and shape of horns**. **Female** differs from previous species by **lack of prominent white stripes** on coat. Seen singly, and is usually a shy and retiring antelope.
Mass: 40 kg

PHIL PERRY

F

Waterbuck
Kobus ellipsiprymnus, Liphiva
Has a restricted distribution in the country, but occurring in most protected areas. Associated with rank grassland interspersed with trees near water. Easily identified by **long shaggy coat, white ring on rump and long inward-curving horns** present only in the male. Male defends a very small patch during the breeding season, the position of which determines his breeding success. "Near Threatened" in the Swazi RDB book.
Mass: 250 kg

PHIL PERRY

SB   **B**

Common reedbuck
Redunca arundinum, Inhlangu
Confined to just a few protected areas including Malolotja, Nisela, Mkhaya and Mlilwane reserves. Favours tall, dense grassy habitats close to water. Identified by **shaggy straw-coloured coat and long horns** in the male. Larger than the next species, with a lighter coat. Seen singly or in small family groups. Lies up in tall grass during the day, more active in the late afternoon and at night. "Near Threatened" in the Swazi RDB book.
Mass: 60 kg

PHIL PERRY

G   **SB**   **B**

Mountain reedbuck
Redunca fulvorufula, Lincala
Regularly sighted only at Malolotja, but also present at Mlawula and Mlilwane reserves. Associated with hilly terrain. Prefers grassland on steep to very steep slopes with rock or woody plant cover. **Male** told from the grey rhebok by the curving **horns**, which are absent in the female. The **female has a shaggier coat and longer ears** than that of the female grey rhebok. "Near Threatened" in the Swazi RDB book.
Mass: 30 kg

PHIL PERRY

G   **L**

Birds

Swaziland has a spectacular array of birds: these range from the largest in the world, the ostrich, to tiny jewel-like sunbirds. There are spectacular densities of vultures and eagles as well as a rich variety of song-birds. To date 500 species have been recorded in the country, these represent over half the species that occur in southern Africa. The vast majority of these species can be seen from within the nation's parks and reserves. However, many populations are in decline and several species have disappeared from the country, currently 40 species are considered at risk of extinction.

Generally birds are quite selective in their choice of habitat and few species are found throughout the country. If one's aim is to see as many species as possible, then a visit to the eastern savanna region is a must – around 100 species can be seen in a single day in the Mlawula, Mbuluzi and Hlane reserves, whilst Hlane also has numerous raptors.

By contrast a visit to the montane grasslands at Malolotja Nature Reserve, though not as productive in terms of numbers, can be just as rewarding - for this is where the endemics occur. Swaziland has no endemics of its own, but some 52 species of southern African endemics occur in the country. Malolotja has one of the most threatened birds in southern Africa, the blue swallow. For the serious birder a visit to scarp or montane forest is a must, but this does require patience and an ear for bird calls as forest species are often furtive and retiring. There are accessible forests at Malolotja and Mlawula Nature Reserves.

Approximately half of all bird species recorded in Swaziland are presented in this section, including nearly all the common birds likely to be seen during a short stay. For further reading and identification, recommended books include Sinclair et al. (2001), and Hockey et al. (2005).

PHIL PERRY

SB **B**

Ostrich
Struthio camelus, Inshi
Occurs only in protected areas and game farms in the bushveld regions. Swazi population is descended from domesticated birds. Eats a variety of plant parts including leaves, flowers and seeds. May live up to 40 years. Eggs are laid in a nest on the ground and are incubated by both male and female. It is the **largest living bird** in the world.

Height: 2 m

MARK D ANDERSON

SB **B** **L**

Crested francolin
Dendroperdix sephaena, Sikhwehle
Occurs widely in bushveld regions. Prefers thickets and bush-encroached savanna, but also occurs in more open habitats. Easily identified by **reddish legs, black bill and white eye stripe**. Usually seen singly or in pairs. Nests on the ground in tall grass.

Length: 33 cm

Natal spurfowl
Pternistis natalensis, Lingagolu/Sikhwehle
Occurs in well-wooded habitats in the montane grassland and bushveld regions. Shows a preference for riparian vegetation, from where it often emits its characteristic loud, screeching call. Identified by **red legs and red bill**. Usually seen singly or in pairs. Nests on the ground concealed by dense vegetation.

MARK D ANDERSON

Length: 35 cm

G SB B L F

Swainson's spurfowl
Pternistis swainsonii, Likwelekwele
Widespread in the montane grassland region, localized in the bushveld regions. Favours tall grass in open situations, and is common in cultivated fields where these border natural habitats. Easily identified by **red bill and facial mask, and black legs**. Often vocal at dawn and dusk, when male may perch in the open. Usually in pairs or small family parties. Nests on the ground in dense grass.
Length: 35 cm

PHIL PERRY

G SB B L

Common quail
Coturnix coturnix, Sigwaca
Widespread, but prefers moist, short grasslands. Often seen in cultivated or fallow fields in coveys of up to 20 birds. Sexually dimorphic with males showing a **dark throat and white eye stripe**. Females are duller. Intra-African migrant arriving in large numbers in wet years to breed during summer. A few individuals may over-winter. Nests on the ground in dense vegetation. Call differentiates the harlequin quail, *C. delegorguei*.
Length: 17 cm

C & M STUART

G SB B L W

Crested guineafowl
Guttera edouardi, Sikhankhanka
Restricted to forest and bushveld regions in the far east of the country. Favours riparian vegetation, where it may be seen in flocks of up to 20 individuals. Has extended its Swaziland distribution westwards in past two decades. Told from next species by **dense, curly black feathers on top of the head and crimson eyes**. Nests on the ground in a concealed situation.

PHIL PERRY

Length: 50 cm

F L

(G) (SB) (B) (L)

Helmeted guineafowl
Numida meleagris, Imphangele
Occurs throughout the country. Favours open areas with tall grass, but regularly forages in cultivated fields, especially bordering natural habitats. Told from previous species by **light blue facial skin and lack of feathers** on top of the head. In stable flocks of up to 40 birds. Susceptible to large-scale changes in land use and poisoning, which has caused major declines in parts of South Africa. Nests on the ground in tall grass.
Length: 55 cm

(W)

White-faced duck
Dendrocygna viduata, Indzindzawo
Occurs in bushveld regions, prefering pans and dams with shallow water, fringed by short, emergent vegetation for breeding. Moves to deeper wetlands to moult, when the birds are flightless and susceptible to predation. Identified by **white face, black bill and nape, and chestnut breast**. Told from fulvous duck, *D. bicolor,* by white face. Usually seen in flocks of up to 200 individuals. Nests on the ground in dense vegetation.
Length: 47 cm

(W)

Egyptian goose
Alopochen aegyptiaca, Lidada
Occurs in wetlands throughout the country, favouring large water bodies with open shorelines. Frequently feeds in agricultural fields, where it is often considered a pest. Identified by **large size, rufous body and face, and red bill**. Seen singly or in pairs during the breeding season, but may form large flocks in winter months when moulting. Nests in a variety of sites, including on the ground, in abandoned raptor nests, or on cliffs.
Length: 65 cm

(W)

Spur-winged goose
Plectropterus gambensis, Injigi
Occurs in wetlands throughout the country. Breeds in secluded wetlands with fringing vegetation, but favours large water bodies for moulting. Identified by **very large size, predominantly black body with red legs and bill**. Seen singly or in pairs during the breeding season, but may form flocks of up to 50 birds in winter months when moulting. May nest on the ground, in a tree hole or an abandoned raptor or hamerkop nest.
Length: 90 cm

Comb duck

Sarkidiornis melanotos

Occurs in wetlands in the bushveld regions. Breeding pairs prefer temporary pans, but moults in larger water bodies. Identified by **large size, dark back, white underparts and black bill**. In males, a **large knob** is present on the upper mandible making identification unmistakable. Usually seen singly or in pairs. Nests in tree hole, which may be re-used in successive years.

Length: 65 cm

African black duck

Anas sparsa, Lidada lemfula

Occurs along perennial rivers throughout the entire country. Favours sections of river with shallow pools lined by dense riparian vegetation. Identified by **dark brown body with conspicuous white marks on back**. Pairs are territorial and defend approximately 4 km of river. Usually takes flight on approach of humans and then flies up or downstream. Nests on ground in river bank in concealed situations.

Length: 55 cm

Yellow-billed duck

Anas undulata

Occurs in wetlands in montane grassland, where it occupies dams, marshes and other open bodies of water. Told from red-billed teal, *A. erythrorhyncha,* by **yellow bill**. Seen in pairs or small groups, but congregates in larger flocks when moulting. Readily hybridizes with the alien invasive mallard duck, *A. playrhynchus*, which threatens the genetic constitution of this species. Nests on the ground in concealed situations.

Length: 57 cm

Southern pochard

Netta erythrophthalma

Generally restricted to wetlands in montane grassland. Prefers deep, clear water bodies where it feeds by diving and rarely comes out onto land. Identified by **dark body, bluish bill and reddish eye**. In Swaziland, only regularly seen at Hawane Dam where small numbers may be present at any time of the year. Undertakes large-scale movements which are poorly understood. Nests in vegetation over water.

Length: 49 cm

SB B L

Greater honeyguide
Indicator indicator, Inhlava
Widely distributed throughout the country, but
generally restricted to wooded habitats. Identified
by **white outer tail feathers and behaviour**.
The territorial call is frequently heard "vic-torr".
Known to lead people and honey badgers to bee
hives, during which the bird becomes agitated and
makes a chattering call. Parasitizes hole-nesting
species such as kingfishers, bee-eaters, barbets
and woodpeckers.
Length: 19 cm

SB B F L

Golden-tailed woodpecker
Campethera abingoni, Incocodzi
Widespread except in open grasslands in the
west. Best identified from other woodpeckers by
call, a loud "waaa". Identified by **heavy streaking on breast and lack of malar stripe**. Male
has a modest red moustache and red cap. Female
lacks moustache and red is restricted to the nape.
Usually seen in pairs, foraging for insects on
branches of trees by "drilling" holes in typical
woodpecker fashion. Nests in holes in trees.
Length: 20 cm

G

Ground woodpecker
Geocolaptes olivaceus
Restricted to the montane grasslands in the west.
Only woodpecker with **plain pinkish or reddish breast and entirely terrestrial habit**.
Forages for ants on the ground in amongst rocks
and rocky outcrops. Lives in pairs or small family groups. Nests in burrows in vertical earth walls
such as in dongas and river cuttings. The burrow
is less than 10 cm in diameter and may reach a
depth of 1 m.
Length: 25 cm

SB B F L

Cardinal woodpecker
Dendropicos fuscescens, Incocodzi
Occurs widely throughout the country except in
open grasslands in the west. Smallest woodpecker in Swaziland, but best identified by **heavily streaked beast and black malar stripe**. Male
has red crown, female black crown. Forages by
tapping for insects in branches of trees. Nests in
holes in trees. When two offspring fledge from
one nest, one will follow the male and the other
the female on separate foraging paths.
Length: 15 cm

Bearded woodpecker
Dendropicos namaquus
Occurs in the low-lying bushveld regions in the east. Identified by **barred (not streaked) breast, black malar stripe and black patches through eyes**. Male has red crown, female black crown. Largest woodpecker in Swaziland. Drums by tapping on dead wood as a means of communication, associated with territorial display and mating. Nests in hole in dead branch which has characteristic oval entrance.
Length: 24 cm

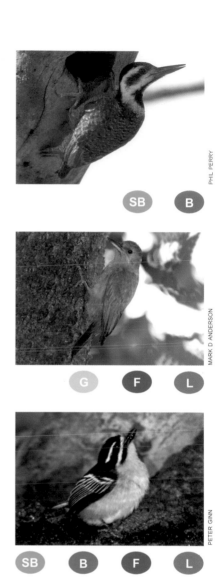

SB B

Olive woodpecker
Dendropicos griseocephalus
Restricted to high-altitude forest and edge habitats in the west and highest peaks in the Lebombos in the east. Identified by **plain olive-green upper and under parts**. Male has red crown, female has grey crown. Usually forages in pairs. May enter gardens in highveld towns, but easily overlooked when not calling. Nests in hole in dead branch.

Length: 20 cm

G F L

Yellow-rumped tinkerbird
Pogoniulus bilineatus
Occurs in the northern bushveld regions where it is most commonly seen in riparian forest along rivers and streams. Identified by **uniform black and white stripes on face.** Makes a monotonous "tok-tok-tok-tok" call with regular pauses after 4-6 notes. Usually seen singly or in pairs. Easily overlooked even when calling. Eats fruit and insects. Nests in hole in dead branch or trunk which it excavates.
Length: 12 cm

SB B F L

Black-collared barbet
Lybius torquatus, Sibagobe/Yimvu
Occurs throughout the country except the highest parts of the montane grasslands. Associated with wooded habitats, and habitually enters towns and cities. Easily identified by **red forehead, face and throat which is lined by a black band**. Male and female participate in antiphonal duet which sounds as if emitted from a single bird. Feeds on fruit and insects. Nests are often excavated in upright or underside of sloping trunk.
Length: 20 cm

G SB B F L

GERHARD GELDENHUYS

Crested barbet

Trachyphonus vaillantii, Ludvonca

Occurs in wooded habitats throughout the country, but avoiding open montane grasslands. Most abundant in open *Acacia* savanna. Identified by **black and white upper parts, yellow under parts and prominent pointed crest**. Very vocal, emitting a long, monotonous trill that may last 30 seconds. Feeds on fruit and insects. Nests are excavated in dead trunk. May rear three or four broods per year.

Length: 23 cm

PHIL PERRY

Southern yellow-billed hornbill

Tockus leucomelas, Umkhotfo

Occurs widely in the low-lying bushveld regions where it is abundant in *Acacia* savanna. Easily identified by **large, yellow banana-shaped beak**. The similar red-billed hornbill *T. erythrorhynchus* has a bright red beak and has a restricted distribution in Swaziland. Nests are built in holes in trees. As in many hornbills, female is sealed within the nest cavity for the duration of incubation. Male provisions female and later the nestlings.

Length: 50 cm

PHIL PERRY

Crowned hornbill

Tockus alboterminatus

Widespread throughout the bushveld regions, avoiding montane grasslands. Associated with riparian forest and forest edge, but does also enter mature woodland. Identified by **uniform brown upper parts and chest, white belly and deep orange or red beak**. Like most hornbills, it eats a variety of food including fruits, insects and lizards. Nests in tree cavity which it cannot excavate itself.

Length: 52 cm

PHIL PERRY

African grey hornbill

Tockus nasutus

Occurs widely but sparsely in the eastern bushveld regions where it is most frequently seen in open savanna. Avoids densely wooded habitats. Identified by **greyish-brown upper and under parts and a conspicuous white line through the eye**. Male has upper bill two-toned yellow and black; female has yellow upper bill. In pairs when breeding but may form small nomadic flocks in the dry season. Nests in tree cavity.

Length: 45 cm

Trumpeter hornbill

Bycanistes bucinator, Mkhontfowemahlatsi
Patchily distributed, but predominantly in the
Lebombos and northern bushveld regions.
Associated with well wooded habitats including
riparian forest. Identified by **large size, black upper parts and chest, white belly and very large
casque on upper bill**. Frequently heard before
seen. Has characteristic call resembling a baby's
wail. Nests in tree cavity.

Length: 60 cm

VICTOR ROBERTS

B   F   L

African hoopoe

Upupa africana, Bhuphuphu
Widespread throughout the country. Present in
most habitats, but avoids closed woodland and
forest. Most abundant in open savanna with short
grass. Easily identified by **rufous upper and under parts, black and white wings, prominent
rufous crest and thin long beak**. Forages mostly
on the ground where it probes for insects in leaf
litter and the soil. Nests in tree cavity.

Length: 26 cm

PHIL PERRY

G   SB   B   L

Green wood-hoopoe

Phoeniculus purpureus
Occurs widely in the bushveld regions, associated
with wooded savannas. Requires mature woodland with old trees that may have suitable holes.
Identified by **shiny, dark body with bright red,
long curved beak**. Usually seen in family groups
which cooperate to raise the young of the alpha
male and female. At night, family members roost
communally in tree cavity. Each territory has
multiple cavities used for roosting and nesting.
Length: 33 cm

GEOFF McILLERON, FIREFLY IMAGES

SB   B   F   L

Common scimitarbill

Rhinopomastus cyanomelas
Occurs throughout the bushveld regions, where
it is most frequently sighted in *Acacia* savanna. Identified by **smaller size** in relation to previous species, with **sharply curved, black beak**.
Usually seen in pairs or small family groups.
Forages by clambering around the trunk and
branches of large trees, probing under bark and in
cracks for larvae. Nests in cavity.

Length: 26 cm

NEIL GRAY

SB   B

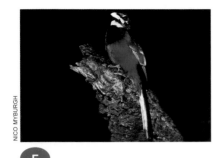

NICO MYBURGH

F

Narina trogon
Apaloderma narina
Sparsely distributed in suitable forest patches throughout the country. May occur in a variety of forests including montane, scarp and riparian forest. Unmistakable with **bright green upper parts and chest, and red under parts**. More frequently heard than seen. Utters a series of mournful hoots. Forages by sallying from a perch to capture insect and returning to perch. Nests in natural tree cavity.
Length: 32 cm

GERHARD GELDENHUYS

SB   **B**

European roller
Coracias garrulus, Ifefe
Occurs as a non-breeding migrant to the bushveld regions, where it may be seen between November and March. It favours open savanna, where it commonly perches on telephone and electricity lines. It can be distinguished from the next species by **blue throat and chest**. Before the return migration, it may form large flocks.

Length: 31 cm

PHIL PERRY

SB   **B**

Lilac-breasted roller
Coracias caudatus, Ifefe
Occurs in eastern parts of the bushveld regions. Like the previous species, it favours open savanna and during summer months the two roller species may be seen perched side-by-side on telephone lines. Distinguished from the previous species by its **purple throat and chest**. It does not migrate, instead pairs defend a territory. Male performs spectacular aerial displays which increase in frequency during breeding season. Nests in cavities.
Length: 28 cm

GERHARD GELDENHUYS

W

Malachite kingfisher
Alcedo cristata, Sipholoti
Widespread and closely associated with wetlands. It may be seen at the edge of dams, rivers and marshes with fringing vegetation such as reeds. Identified by **small size, shiny blue upper parts extending to the head, bright orange upper parts, red beak and lack of orange eye stripe**. Catches fish by searching from perch and darting into water, returning to perch to swallow. Nests in tunnel excavated in bank such as river cutting.
Length: 14 cm

African pygmy-kingfisher
Ispidina picta
Occurs widely but patchily as an intra-African migrant. May be seen from October to April in a variety of habitats, but mostly in forest, forest edge including riparian, but rarely seen at water's edge. Similar to previous species in having shiny blue upper parts, orange under parts and red beak, but distinguished by **orange stripe above eye**. Feeds on insects and small vertebrates; does not catch fish. Nests in tunnel in earth bank.
Length: 13 cm

Woodland kingfisher
Halcyon senegalensis, Imbobolukhahlu
Occurs as an intra-African migrant in the northern bushveld regions; sparsely in the south. Present between November and March. Associated with mature woodland, avoiding scrubby thornveld. Identified by **brilliant blue upper parts, black shoulder patch, light blue-grey under parts extending to the head, and two toned beak**. Call is loud and characteristic "whit-trrrrrrrrrrrrrr". Nests in natural cavity or disused barbet hole.
Length: 23 cm

Brown-hooded kingfisher
Halcyon albiventris Sipholoti
Widespread throughout the country. Present in a variety of wooded habitats including gardens, avoiding extensive grasslands and closed forest. Similar to next species from which it is distinguished by l**arger size, all-red beak, blue in wing and shoulder and lack of white collar**. Preys on insects and small vertebrates which it hunts in typical sit-and-wait fashion. Nests in tunnel excavated in earth bank.
Length: 23 cm

Striped kingfisher
Halcyon chelicuti
Occurs in bushveld regions. Associated with savanna habitats, but most abundant in *Acacia* savanna. Similar to previous species, but is **smaller, has blackish upper bill and red lower bill, no blue in wing or shoulder when perched and a whitish collar** that runs from below the eye across the back of the neck. Usually seen singly or in pairs. Feeds mostly on insects. Nests in tree cavity.
Length: 18 cm

GERHARD GELDENHUYS

Giant kingfisher
Megaceryle maximus
Occurs patchily throughout the country. Closely associated with water, and may be seen at larger dams and rivers. **Large size and chestnut under parts** render it unmistakable. Male has chestnut on breast, female on belly and vent. Usually seen in pairs. Preys on fish which it mostly catches by flying from perch. May hover, but only for short spells. Nests in excavated tunnel in earth bank.

Length: 45 cm

PHIL PERRY

W

Pied kingfisher
Ceryle rudis, Linombe
Widespread in suitable wetland habitats preferring larger rivers and dams lacking dense riparian forest. Medium-sized kingfisher with entirely **black-and-white plumage**. Male has second narrow breast band below main band; female lacks second band and main band usually incomplete. Captures fish either from a perch or by hovering. Nests colonially in tunnel in bank. An extra male often assists pairs in provisioning the nestlings.
Length: 27 cm

PHIL PERRY

SB   **B**

White-fronted bee-eater
Merops bullockoides
Occurs at only a few sites where it may be readily seen such as Mlilwane Game Reserve. Usually present in woodland or savanna near water. Easily identified by **red throat, white chin, white forehead, green upper parts and cinnamon breast**. Sallies in typical bee-eater fashion. Catches flying insects from a perch, often returning to perch to consume prey. Nests colonially in tunnels in earth bank.
Length: 23 cm

PHIL PERRY

G   **SB**   **B**   **L**

Little bee-eater
Merops pusillus
Widespread in the country. Associated with a variety of habitats including savanna and forest edge. May occur in grasslands where at least a few trees are present. Identified by **small size, yellow throat, black breast band, buff under parts and green upper parts**. Hawks insects in typical bee-eater style. Usually seen singly or in pairs, but may roost in small groups. Nests in tunnel in bank.
Length: 18 cm

European bee-eater

Merops apiaster, Umhlolamvula/Lihlolamvula
Occurs as a non-breeding migrant throughout the
country. May be seen between October and April.
Congregates in very large flocks just before return
migration to Europe, often circling overhead and
calling continuously. Identified by **blue under
parts, yellow throat and golden upper parts**.
Flocks often perch on telephone lines. A small
population has started breeding in South Africa.

Length: 27 cm

PETER GINN

G   SB   B   L

Speckled mousebird

Colius striatus, Indlati
Widespread and adapted to edge habitats.
Requires some cover such as thickets, tangles and
gardens. Identified by **uniform grey-brown colouring and very long tail**. Distinguished from
next species by lack of red on face and legs. Lives
in small flocks. Forages for fruit by clambering
through tree like a mouse. Drops body temperature on cold nights. Flight appears laboured. Nest
is an untidy cup, hidden in thicket.
Length: 33 cm

PHIL PERRY

G   SB   B   F   L

Red-faced mousebird

Urocolius indicus, Umntjivovo/Lishilolo
Occurs widely in the bushveld regions.
Associated with a variety of habitats, but most
frequently seen in *Acacia* savanna. Distinguished
from previous species by **red face and red legs**.
Similar in habits to previous species, living in
flocks and eating fruit. Takes regular dust baths
at traditional sites which may be used over many
years. Flight is fast and direct. Nest is an untidy
cup, hidden in thicket.
Length: 32 cm

GERHARD GELDENHUYS

SB   B   L

Jacobin cuckoo

Clamator jacobinus, Inkanku
Occurs as an intra-African migrant in the bushveld regions. Associated with savanna and woodland habitats where it may be seen between
November and March. Identified by **black upper
parts and pure white underparts**. Distinguished
from Levaillant's cuckoo, *Clamator levaillantii,*
by unstreaked under parts. Parasitises the dark-
capped bulbul and fork-tailed drongo.

Length: 34 cm

MARK D ANDERSON

SB   B

SB · B · F · L

Red-chested cuckoo

Cuculus solitarius, Pezukwemkhono
A widespread intra-African migrant. Associated with wooded situations such as forest, forest edge, dense woodland, gardens and exotic plantations. Best identified by **call "piet-my-vrou"**, which is heard October to January. Has **plain grey-brown upper parts, barred under parts with orange breast**. Inconspicuous when not calling, typically sitting still high up in a tall tree. Parasitises a variety of robins, chats and thrushes.
Length: 29 cm

SB · B · F · L

Black cuckoo

Cuculus clamosus
Occurs as an intra-African migrant throughout the country. Associated with similar habitat to previous species. Best identified by **call "hoop-hoo hoooooooo"**, heard from October to January. Distinguished from other cuckoos by **entirely black plumage**. Differs from black cuckooshrike by lack of yellow in gape. Difficult to spot when silent. Parasitises *Laniarius* shrikes, which in Swaziland only includes the southern boubou.
Length: 30 cm

SB · B · F · L

Klaas's cuckoo

Chrysococcyx klaas
Occurs throughout in a wide range of habitats including woodland, forest edge, exotic plantations and riparian forest. Male identified by **shiny green upper parts, white under parts and small white patch behind eye**. Female is duller with finely barred brown under parts. Conspicuous when calling during the breeding season, but difficult to detect in the dry winter months. Parasitises batises, warblers and sunbirds.
Length: 18 cm

SB · F · L

African emerald cuckoo

Chrysococcyx cupreus
Occurs widely but patchily. Associated with forest, forest edge and mature woodland. Mostly an intra-African migrant, but some birds over-winter. Male is unmistakable **shiny green on upper parts and on throat, and bright yellow under parts**. Female is duller and barred green below. Very difficult to see clearly as it tends to hide in dense vegetation, but its call is loud and distinctive "Pretty Georgie". Paratises camaropteras.
Length: 20 cm

Diderick cuckoo

Chrysococcyx caprius
Occurs as an intra-African migrant throughout the country. Associated with a variety of wooded habitats. Distinguished from Klaas's cuckoo by **call, red eye and white eye stripe** which extends from beak to behind eye. Male has **shiny green upper parts with white spots on wing**. Female is browner. Conspicious and often seen around weaver colonies. Call is a loud "dee dee deeder-ick". Paratises weavers, widowbirds and bishops.
Length: 19 cm

SB   B   F   L

Burchell's coucal

Centropus burchellii, **Umfuku**
Occurs in bushveld and Lebombo regions. Prefers ecotone habitats between forest/woodland and grassland, or rank vegetation near wetlands. Identified by **large size, dark head, back and tail, chestnut wing, red eye and dirty cream under parts**. Creeps through thickets, general-ly low down foraging for insects, frogs, lizards, small mammals and birds. Makes large oval nest with side entrance in rank vegetation or in thicket.
Length: 41 cm

SB   B   L

African palm-swift

Cypsiurus parvus
Patchily distributed throughout the country. May occur in a wide range of habitats but closely as-sociated with exotic palm trees in which it nests. Commonly seen in urban environments where such palms have been planted. Identified by **mouse-brown plumage, slender build and very long, deeply forked tail**. Often circles about in small flocks in vicinity of palms. Unique nest consists of feathers glued with saliva to palm leaf.
Length: 15 cm

G   SB   B   L

African black swift

Apus barbatus
Patchily distributed but frequents northern mon-tane grasslands. Closely associated with cliffs, on which it nests during early summer. A **larg-ish, uniformly dark** swift. In good light may be distinguished from very similar non-breeding mi-grant common swift, *A. apus,* by contrasting **dark brown back and paler secondaries**. Usually seen flying in large, noisy flocks. Nest consists of feathers glued to rock crevice on cliff face.
Length: 18 cm

G   L

53

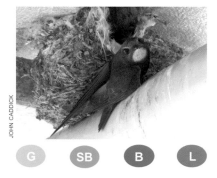

JOHN CADDICK

Little swift
Apus affinis
Widespread and often nests on man-made structures. Identified by **dark plumage, broad white band on rump and squarish tail**. Highly gregarious in large flocks of up to hundreds of birds. Most colonies disappear for two months in midwinter, presumably migrating north. Builds messy nest from feathers and grass glued with saliva to underside of bridge or eaves of building. Breeds colonially or in small groups.
Length: 13 cm

(G) (SB) (B) (L)

NEIL GRAY

White-rumped swift
Apus caffer
Widespread as an intra-African migrant. Not restricted to any particular habitat. Distinguished from previous species by **narrow white band on rump and deeply forked tail**. The similar horus swift, *Apus horus,* has broad white rump with shallow forked tail. Usually seen singly or in pairs, often mixing in flocks of other swifts. Nests in crevice on cliff, but regularly takes over nest of swallow, lining the entrance with feathers.
Length: 15 cm

(G) (SB) (B) (L)

PHIL PERRY

Purple-crested turaco
Gallirex porphyreolophus, Ligwalagwala
Widespread in bushveld and Lebombo regions in well-wooded habitats including various types of forest, dense woodland and forest-savanna ecotone. Avoids open grasslands. Identified by **large size, green under parts, deep blue upper parts, bright red wings**. Distinguished from other green turacos by **purple crest and black beak**. Seen singly or in pairs. Builds large messy nest in tree. Swaziland's national bird.
Length: 42 cm

(SB) (B) (F) (L)

PHIL PERRY

Grey go-away-bird
Corythaixoides concolor, Umkuwe
Sparsely distributed in the eastern bushveld region. Occurs in savanna habitats dominated by *Acacia* species. Easily identified by **all-grey plumage and prominent crest**. Very vocal giving a characteristic loud "kwee". Rumoured to warn other animals of human presence, hence its English name. Seen singly or in pairs, rarely in small flocks. Builds a messy nest in thorny tree.

Length: 48 cm

(B)

Barn owl
Tyto alba, Ingovazana
Widespread in almost any habitat, but avoids deep forest. Usually closely associated with suitable nest site, which is crevice or crack in cliff; but has adapted to human habitation frequently nesting in chimneys or barns. Identified by **sandy-brown upper parts, pale under parts and facial "mask"**. Characteristic screeching call heard throughout the year. Does not build nest, but lays eggs directly on rock face or building.
Length: 32 cm

G SB B L

African scops-owl
Otus senegalensis, Sikhovana
Occurs in the eastern bushveld region. Associated with mature *Acacia* savanna. Identified by **small size and prominent ear tufts**. Frequently heard uttering crisp "krup" in suitable habitat. Catches insects such as grasshoppers which it plucks off the ground. Nests in natural cavity in tree. Roosts in traditional sites on side branch of large tree.

Length: 19 cm

B

Spotted eagle-owl
Bubo africanus, Sikhova
Occurs sparsely throughout the country. Associated with a variety of habitats including grassland, savanna, riparian forest and urban areas. Identified by **large size, mottled brown plumage and yellow eyes**. The similar Cape eagle-owl, *Bubo capensis,* has deep orange eyes. Feeds on rodents, birds and reptiles. Nests in cracks in cliffs, which may be re-used in successive years.
Length: 45 cm

G SB B L

Pearl-spotted owlet
Glaucidium perlatum, Makobogwane
Occurs only in *Acacia* savanna in the eastern bushveld region. Identified by **small size, lack of ear tufts, streaked breast and black "eye spots"** on back of head. The similar African barred owlet, *Glaucidium capense*, has barred breast. Frequently seen during the day when mobbed by birds. Call is a characteristic "tieeu tieeu tieeu" rising in volume and ending in descending "pooi pooi". Nests in natural tree cavity.
Length: 18 cm

B

PHIL PERRY

Marsh owl
Asio capensis, Ingovazana
Sparsely distributed in the country. Closely associated with rank grassland or marshes. Identified by **dark brown upper parts, paler under parts, dark band around eyes and black beak**. Rests by day on the ground in dense, tall grass. Often observed flying singly or in pairs over marsh before sunset. Nest is scrape on the ground, well hidden in tall grass. A "roof" is created by weaving tufts of grass above nest.
Length: 37 cm.

ARA MONADJEM

Fiery-necked nightjar
Caprimulgus pectoralis
Widespread in a wide range of open habitats such as grassland, savanna and woodland, but absent from the northern montane grasslands. Best identified by **call which is a trilled whistle** "good lord deliver us". Distinguished from next species by **call, more extensive white patches in tail and habitat**. Frequently seen singly sitting on dirt roads at night. Eggs are laid in a scrape on bare ground, and blend in by cryptic colouration.
Length: 24 cm

GEOFF McILLERON, FIREFLY IMAGES

Freckled nightjar
Caprimulgus tristigma, Malwelwe/Bhabhodi
Occurs sparsely in appropriate habitat throughout the country. Closely associated with rocky outcrops and boulder-strewn hill slopes. Best identified by **call, a loud double-noted "bao waow"**. Distinguished from previous species by **less white in the tail**. Infrequently seen, but may be vocal throughout the year. Eggs are laid directly on a flat rock face, and blend in perfectly by cryptic colouration.
Length: 28 cm

GINA JC WILGENBUS

African olive-pigeon
Columba arquatrix
Occurs in montane grasslands in wooded habitats, including exotic plantations. Identified by **speckled purplish-brown plumage with yellow eye patch, beak and legs**. Seen in small groups when it can easily be overlooked due to quiet disposition. Shy, flying off when disturbed. Feeds on fruit, including exotic *Solanum mauritianum* whose seeds it helps disperse. Nest is untidy platform of twigs, high up in forest tree.
Length: 40 cm

Laughing dove
Streptopelia senegalensis
Occurs widely in the bushveld and Lebombo regions. Associated with a variety of habitats including savanna, woodland, fallow fields and urban areas. Avoids open grassland and forest. Identified by **plain pinkish-brown plumage and lack of black neck ring**. Locally very abundant. Feeds on seeds which it consumes on the ground. Present in pairs or small flocks. Builds a flimsy nest, usually low down in a tree.
Length: 25 cm

SB　B　L

Cape turtle-dove
Streptopelia capicola, Lituba
Occurs throughout the country. May be seen in almost any situation except in deep forest interior. Identified by **greyish plumage and obvious neck ring**. Distinguished from next species by **smaller size and dark eye**. Seen singly, in pairs or in flocks numbering hundreds of birds. Forages on the ground for seeds. Nest is a flimsy platform of twigs through which the eggs can often be seen from below.
Length: 27 cm

G　SB　B　L

Red-eyed dove
Streptopelia semitorquata
Widespread and in almost any habitat but prefers more wooded situations than the previous species. Identified by **greyish plumage and obvious neck ring**. Distinguished from previous species by **larger size, red eye, pinkish wash on breast and broad greyish band on tail tip**. Seen singly, in pairs or small flocks. Forages on the ground for seeds, but often seen perched high up in a tree. Nest is a flimsy platform of twigs.
Length: 35 cm

SB　B　F　L

Emerald-spotted wood-dove
Turtur chalcospilos, Sigulugwane
Widespread but avoids the higher montane grasslands to the west. Seen in a range of savanna and woodland habitats. Also present in riparian forest, but avoids forest interior. Identified by **brownish upper parts, paler under parts, greyish head and green spots on wing**. Call is one of the characteristic sounds of the bushveld, a mournful "hoo hoo hoo hoo tu-tu-tu-tu-tu". Eggs are laid in a flimsy nest low down on a tree stump or branch.
Length: 20 cm

SB　B　L

GEOFF McILLERON, FIREFLY IMAGES

SB **F** **L**

Tambourine dove
Turtur tympanistria
Widespread in appropriate habitat. Associated with closed woodland and forest, but particularly common in riparian forest. Best identified by **call** which is similar to the previous species, but at a slower pace and more drawn out. Easily overlooked when not calling. Distinguished from previous species by **darker upper parts, whitish under parts, white eye stripe and lack of wing spots**. Nest similar to previous species.
Length: 22 cm

PHIL PERRY

SB **B** **F**

African green-pigeon
Treron calvus, Litubantfontfo
Occurs throughout the bushveld regions, and absent from montane grasslands. Most frequently seen in well-wooded habitats including riparian forest and the forest-savanna ecotone. Identified by **green plumage, red legs and red and white beak**. Often seen feeding in fruiting tree, where it may assemble in small groups. Nest is flimsy platform of twigs, usually high up in tall tree.

Length: 29 cm

MIKE UNWIN

G

Denham's bustard
Neotis denhami, Inseme
Occurs only at Malolotja Nature Reserve; vagrant elsewhere in the montane grassland region. Closely tied to good quality, undegraded grasslands. Identified by l**arge size, brownish upper parts, pale under parts and black and white markings on wing**. Seen singly or in pairs, walking through grassland searching for insect and small vertebrate prey. Nests on the ground. Listed as "Endangered" in the Swazi RDB.
Length: 105 cm

PHIL PERRY

G **SB** **B**

Black-bellied bustard
Lissotis melanogaster, Umfumbane
Widespread in suitable habitat. Usually seen in tall or dense grass in bushveld or montane grassland regions. Identified by **light brown upper parts with black markings**. Male has black belly with thin black line running up the neck to the throat. Female has whitish belly. Distinguished from red-crested korhaan, *Lophotis ruficrista*, by longer legs, markings on upper parts and black line from throat to belly. Nests on the ground.
Length: 62 cm

Black crake

Amaurornis flavirostris, Inkhukhumazana
Occurs in suitable habitat throughout the country, but rare at higher altitudes, especially in the south. Closely associated with wetlands, where it frequents reed beds. Easily identified by **all black plumage, red legs, red eye, and greenish beak**. Not as skulking as other rails and crakes and can be observed relatively easily. Walks on the ground through reeds and water's edge searching for insects. Nests low down in reed bed.
Length: 22 cm

Common moorhen

Gallinula chloropus
Sparsely distributed in wetlands. Prefers water bodies fringed with reed beds or rank vegetation. Identified by **sooty-black plumage, white markings on the side, red head shield and yellow tip to beak**. Distinguished from smaller lesser moorhen, *G. angulata,* by red base to beak and lack of red from top to tip of beak. Usually seen swimming on edge of dense vegetation. Nests in dense vegetation above water level.
Length: 33 cm

Red-knobbed coot

Fulica cristata
Occurs in montane grassland region on large water bodies at higher altitudes. Identified by **black plumage, white head shield and beak**. Head shield has two characteristic **red knobs** at its back end. Usually swims well away from the edge of water body and may form large flocks outside of breeding season. Feeds mostly on aquatic vegetation which it may dive for. Nest is floating mass of plant material, anchored to aquatic vegetation.
Length: 43 cm

Common greenshank

Tringa nebularia
Widespread in suitable wetland habitats. A non-breeding summer migrant, preferring shallow water and mud flats. Identified by **greyish-brown upper parts, pale under parts, long green legs and long beak**. Distinguished from the similar marsh sandpiper, *T. stagnatilis,* by more robust beak and larger size. Probes in shallow water and mud for insects. Flies off strongly when disturbed, calling and showing white back and rump.
Length: 34 cm

PHIL PERRY

Wood sandpiper
Tringa glareola
Occurs widely throughout the country in suitable wetland habitats, where it is present as non-breeding summer migrant. Associated with shallow water, mud flats and rivers. Identified by **brownish upper parts which are spotted white and yellowish legs**. Distinguished from next species by white rump and lack of white shoulder patch. Probes in shallow water and mud for insects.

Length: 20 cm

PHIL PERRY

Common sandpiper
Actitis hypoleucos
Occurs as a non-breeding summer migrant throughout the country. Associated with a wide variety of wetland habitats including shores of dams, rivers and marshes. Identified by **dark brown upper parts, white under parts and white shoulder patch**. Has habit of "wagging" its tail in the typical style of wagtails. Probably the most frequently sighted sandpiper in the country, where it is seen singly or in small groups.
Length: 19 cm

PHIL PERRY

Ruff
Philomachus pugnax
Occurs sparsely as a non-breeding summer migrant throughout the country. Usually seen on unvegetated shore of wetland or on mudflat. Identified by **dumpy body, scaled upper parts and robust beak**. Legs may be orange or dark brown. Male is noticeably larger than female. Often forms small flocks of 10 – 20 birds.

Length: 31 cm

GERHARD GELDENHUYS

African jacana
Actophilornis africanus
Occurs in the east in wetlands with floating vegetation such as water lilies. Identified by **rich chestnut brown upper and under parts, black neck, white throat and blue head shield and beak**. Much larger than lesser jacana, *Microparra capensis*. Has very long toes for walking on floating vegetation, foraging for insects. Female lays eggs for multiple males. Incubating and provisioning of young entirely by male.
Length: 27 cm

Water thick-knee
Burhinus vermiculatus, Kelkelwane
Occurs in suitable wetland habitats throughout the country. Frequently seen along large rivers and dams with open, sandy shores. Appears **brownish with long legs and big head**. Distinguished from next species by **white wing bar**. Often in small groups of up to 10 – 15 birds. Call loud and characteristic cry "ti-ti-ti-ti-teee-teee-teee-ti-teee". Nest is a simple scrape on sandy ground.

Length: 39 cm

Spotted thick-knee
Burhinus capensis, Umnkonkoni
Widespread in suitable grassland, fallow fields or open savanna habitats. Frequently seen along dirt roads at night. Appears **speckled brown with long legs and big head**. Distinguished from previous species by **lack of white wing bar**. Frequently seen singly or in pairs. Call similar to previous species but more musical. Eggs are laid on the ground in short grassland, where cryptic eggs are well camouflaged.
Length: 44 cm

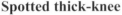

Black-winged stilt
Himantopus himantopus
Occurs sparsely in suitable wetlands. Closely associated with shallow water and open shorelines. Easily identified by **black-and-white plumage, long red legs and long black beak**. Wades singly or in small groups in water where it probes for insects in the mud. Eggs are laid in a scrape on the ground which is lined with twigs and grass.

Length: 38 cm

Three-banded plover
Charadrius tricollaris
Occurs in suitable wetland habitats throughout the country. Frequents open shorelines of rivers, dams and other water bodies. Identified by **dark upper parts, pale under parts, red legs and beak, and two clear black breast bands**. Seen foraging singly or in pairs on shoreline where it pecks insects off the surface. Eggs are laid in a shallow scrape on the ground, often lined with stones.
Length: 18 cm

Blacksmith lapwing
Vanellus armatus
Widespread in suitable habitat. Associated with short grassland or shoreline, often on the edge of wetlands. Easily identified by **black-and-white plumage with grey wings**. Usually in pairs or small flocks, where it forages on the ground for insects. Very noisy when disturbed, taking off and circling above uttering metallic "tink-tink-tink". Nests on the ground, frequently on lawns where eggs can be destroyed by lawn-mowers.
Length: 30 cm

African wattled lapwing
Vanellus senegallus, Ligwegwezi
Occurs in suitable habitat throughout the country. Associated with short grassland on the edge of wetlands. Identified by **uniform grey-brown upper and under parts, yellow legs, yellow beak with black tip and white forehead**. Has characteristic **wattles at base of beak**. Seen in pairs or small flocks, which are vocal when disturbed. Eggs are laid on the ground. Chicks leave the nest soon after hatching.
Length: 35 cm

Black-winged lapwing
Vanellus melanopterus
Occurs throughout the montane grassland regions, and regularly seen at Malolotja Nature Reserve. Prefers short grassland, moving to burnt or heavily grazed areas when grass grows too long. Identified by **greyish-brown upper and under parts and white belly**. Distinguished from similar Senegal lapwing, *V. lugubris,* by reddish legs and larger white forehead. Seen in small flocks. Listed as "Near Threatened" in the Swazi RDB.
Length: 27 cm

Crowned lapwing
Vanellus coronatus
May be seen throughout the country, but generally absent in northern parts of montane grassland region. Prefers areas with short grass in a variety of habitats including marshes, grassland, savanna and woodland. Identified by **greyish-brown upper and under parts, red legs and beak**, with a characteristic **black crown bordered by a narrow white and black line**. Usually in small, noisy flocks. Lays eggs on the ground.
Length: 30 cm

Black-shouldered kite

Elanus caeruleus, Loheya/Lohheyane

Widespread preferring open habitats and avoiding dense woodland, bush-encroached savanna and forest. Most commonly sighted on Swazi Nation Land. Identified by **grey upper parts, white under parts and black shoulder patch**. Probably the most abundant raptor breeding in Swaziland. Feeds on rodents and numbers fluctuate according to prey populations. Nests on flat-crowned tree, raising up to 3 young per breeding attempt.
Length: 30 cm

GERHARD GELDENHUYS

G **SB** **B** **L**

Black kite

Milvus migrans, Umkhowa

Widespread in a variety of habitats, avoiding only dense woodland and forest. Identified by **uniform brown plumage with yellow beak and forked tail** (yellow-billed kite, *M.m.parasitus*). Rarer subspecies (black kite, *M.m.migrans*) has yellow base to black beak with shallow forked tail. Yellow-billed kite is intra-African migrant, some breeding in Swaziland. Black kite is non-breeding migrant. Nests in main fork of thorny tree.
Length: 55 cm

PHIL PERRY

G **SB** **B** **L**

African fish-eagle

Haliaeetus vocifer, Inkwanzi

Occurs in the eastern parts of the bushveld regions. Closely tied to large water bodies such as dams and rivers. Easily identified by **chestnut upper parts and belly, and white breast and head**. Female obviously larger than male. Call is evocative "Whow-kayow-kwow". Highly territorial. Captures fish from traditional perch overlooking water, swooping down to pluck prey out of the water. Nests in fork of tall tree near water.
Length: 68 cm

PHIL PERRY

W

White-backed vulture

Gyps africanus, Lingce

Occurs patchily in the eastern bushveld. Forages in savanna habitats. Identified by uniform **cream-brown upper and under parts, dark wings and long dark neck that lacks feathers**. Told from similar Cape vulture, *G. coprotheres*, by smaller size and dark eye. Feeds on carrion, including dead cattle left at "vulture restaurants". Nests in tall, evergreen trees along rivers and drainage lines. Listed as "Near Threatened" in Swazi RDB.
Length: 95 cm

Immature

PHIL PERRY

B

PHIL PERRY

B

Lappet-faced vulture
Aegypius tracheliotus, Lingce
Occurs sparsely in the eastern bushveld, breeding only at Hlane National Park. Forages in a variety of savanna habitats, avoiding human disturbance. Has **dark brown plumage, heavy beak, white leg feathers and red wattles** on head and neck. Feeds on carrion. Usually largest vulture at a carcass where it dominates other species. Prefers to nest in canopy of tall, thorny tree away from riparian zone. Listed as "Endangered" in the Swazi RDB.
Length: 100 cm

PHIL PERRY

B

White-headed vulture
Aegypius occipitalis
Occurs sparsely in the eastern bushveld, breeding only at Hlane National Park. Forages in a variety of savanna habitats, avoiding human disturbance. Identified by **dark plumage, white belly and leg feathers, white head and red beak with blue base**. Female differs by white inner flight feathers. Attends carcasses singly or in pairs. Prefers to nest in canopy of tall, thorny tree away from riparian zone. Listed as "Endangered" in the Swazi RDB.
Length: 80 cm

PHIL PERRY

SB   B

Brown snake-eagle
Circaetus cinereus
Occurs sparsely in the bushveld regions. Associated with savanna and woodland habitats. Identified by **uniform brown plumage and large head**. Distinguished from immature of next species by yellow eye. May be observed perched on prominent perch or soaring. Usually seen singly. Feeds on snakes and lizards. Nest is small and located on canopy of tall tree.

Length: 74 cm

PHIL PERRY

B

Bateleur
Terathopius ecaudatus, Ingculungculu
Occurs in the eastern bushveld regions, in savanna habitats. Identified by **black and grey plumage, chestnut nape and red legs and beak**. In flight appears almost tail-less. Female has narrower black terminal band on wings than male. Flies with characteristic non-flapping style, low over savanna searching for carrion. Often first raptor to locate a carcass. Builds a small nest in fork of tall tree. Listed as "Endangered" in the Swazi RDB.
Length: 62 cm

African marsh-harrier
Circus ranivorus
Occurs as a breeding resident only in grasslands to the west of the country. Associated with rank grasslands in marshes. Identified by **uniform dark brown plumage and chestnut thighs**. Usually seen quartering singly or in pairs, low over vegetation in search of rodent prey. Pairs require at least 2 ha of marsh for breeding. Nests on ground in dense patch of grass. Listed as "Vulnerable" in the Swazi RDB.
Length: 46 cm

ADAM RILEY

 W

African harrier-hawk
Polyboroides typus
Occurs widely in the country but scarce in open grasslands to the west. Observed in most wooded situations including riparian forest, forest edge, woodland and savanna. Easily identified by **uniform grey plumage, lightly barred belly and yellow face and legs**. Has long "double-jointed" legs which it uses to pluck nestlings out of tree cavity. Also feeds on reptiles. Nests in fork of tall tree in riparian forest.
Length: 63 cm

Immature

PHIL PERRY

 SB B F L

Lizard buzzard
Kaupifalco monogrammicus, Lusotane
Occurs widely in the bushveld regions, scarcer at higher altitudes to the west. Usually associated with woodland and savanna habitats but also seen in semi-urban environments. Identified by **grey plumage, red beak and legs, and vertical black line through centre of throat**. Call is loud and distinct "klu-klu-klu-klu wooeeee". Often seen perched on prominent structure such as telephone pole from which it captures small vertebrate prey.
Length: 36 cm

WILL NICHOL

SB B

African goshawk
Accipiter tachiro
Widespread and closely associated with well-wooded habitats. Characteristic call "whit whit whit" usually uttered high in the sky. **Darker** than most other *Accipiter* hawks. **Upper parts greyish-brown.** Under parts barred brown in female, grey in male. Performs territorial flight early in the morning. Otherwise inconspicuous and easily overlooked. Nest is small platform of twigs, usually in fork of tall tree in riparian forest.
Length: 38 cm

LEX HES

SB B F L

PETER GINN

B

Shikra
Accipiter badius

Occurs in eastern parts of the bushveld regions. Generally associated with open savanna habitats. Identified by **small size, yellow beak and legs, red eye**, and in flight shows **uniform grey upper tail and rump**. Inconspicuous when not calling, but may sit on prominent perch in tree. Feeds predominantly on reptiles which it catches on the ground. Nest usually situated in riparian forest, but also uses exotic plantations of eucalyptus.

Length: 29 cm

NICO MYBURGH

SB   B   F   L

Black sparrowhawk
Accipiter melanoleucus

Occurs sparsely throughout the country. Closely associated with wooded habitats including forest and woodland, but may be seen flying over open terrain. Easily identified by **uniform black plumage with variable amounts of white on under parts**. Remarkably inconspicuous for a bird of its size when not calling. Feeds mostly on birds. Nest is a large structure typically placed in a high fork in a tall tree, usually in forest or exotic plantation.

Length: 52 cm

PHIL PERRY

G   SB   B   L

Steppe buzzard
Buteo vulpinus

Widespread non-breeding migrant, present between October and March. May be seen in almost any habitat, but avoids forest interior. Identified by **variable brown plumage, yellow base to beak, yellow legs** and inconspicuous and ill-defined **white breast band**. Most frequently seen perched singly on telephone pole, from which it captures rodent prey. May return to same location in successive seasons.

Length: 48 cm

PHIL PERRY

G   L

Jackal buzzard
Buteo rufofuscus, Inhlandlokati

Occurs widely in the montane grasslands and Lebombo Mountains. Absent from bushveld regions in between. Identified by **black upper parts, chestnut breast and vent, and barred belly**. Commonly encountered in suitable habitat where it may perch on telephone pole. Catches rodent prey by waiting from perch. Has a characteristic call reminiscent of that of a jackal. Nests in fork or canopy of tree in forest or forest edge.

Length: 49 cm

Verreauxs' eagle

Aquila verreauxii, Lusoti

Occurs in the montane grasslands to the west. Closely tied to breeding cliffs. Identified by **large size, uniform black plumage, yellow beak and legs, and white back**. Pairs circle over territory which is vigorously defended from other pairs. Dassies, *Provacia capensis*, are staple diet. Nest is a very large structure which may be re-used over many years. Only one chick is raised per annum. Listed as "Vulnerable" in the Swazi RDB.

Length: 84 cm

G

African hawk-eagle

Aquila spilogaster

Occurs in eastern bushveld, savanna habitats. Identified by uniform **black upper parts, white under parts streaked with prominent black markings and white feathered tarsus**. In flight shows white "windows" in upper wing and black terminal band in tail. Often sexes cooperate to hunt prey including game birds. Nest is very large and always placed in fork of tall tree away from riparian forest. "Endangered" in Swazi RDB.

Length: 63 cm

B

Wahlberg's eagle

Aquila wahlbergi

Occurs in the bushveld regions of the country. Associated with a variety of savanna and woodland habitats. Plumage highly variable. Most common morph is uniform dark brown. Speckled morph and pale morph also present. All morphs show characteristic **small crest and feathered tarsus**. Feeds on birds and other small vertebrates. Nest is typically placed in fork of tall tree, usually along drainage line or river.

Length: 57 cm

SB   B   L

Martial eagle

Polemaetus bellicosus, Lusoti

Occurs sparsely in the bushveld in savanna habitats. Is **large with dark brown upper parts and chest, belly and thighs white with dark spots**. Differs from black-chested snake-eagle *Circaetus pectoralis* by larger size, spotted belly and dark under wings. Feeds on vertebrates including hares, game birds and young of small antelope. Large nest is situated high up in tall tree along drainage line. "Vulnerable" in the Swazi RDB.

Length: 81 cm

B

GERHARD GELDENHUYS

Long-crested eagle
Lophaetus occipitalis, Lusoti

Occurs patchily throughout the country. May be seen in a variety of habitats, but prefers the eco-tone between forest and grassland. Easily identified by uniform **dark brown plumage and very long crest on head**. Often perches on telephone poles from where it hunts rodent prey. Nest is placed high up in fork of tall tree. Listed as "Near Threatened" in the Swazi RDB.

Length: 55 cm

DUNCAN BUTCHART

African crowned eagle
Stephanoaetus coronatus, Lusoti

Occurs patchily in forest habitats. Identified by **very large size, dark upper parts, mottled black and white under parts**. In flight shows conspicuous **chestnut under wing**. Performs spectacular aerial displays calling "kewee-kewee-kewee". Highly territorial. Male and female may cooperate to hunt monkeys and small antelope. Nest, in fork of tall forest tree, may be re-used over many years. "Vulnerable" in Swazi RDB.

Length: 85 cm

PHIL PERRY

Rock kestrel
Falco rupicolus

Widespread in suitable habitat, but mostly absent from flat, low-lying areas in the east. Associated with nesting cliffs. Identified by **rufous plumage marked with black spots and black wings**. Male has grey head, rump and tail. Female has dark brown head. Distinguished from lesser kestrel, *F. naumanni,* by more robust build and lack of salmon-pink or white on under parts. Feeds on rodents. Eggs laid directly on rocky ledge on cliff.

Length: 31 cm

PHIL PERRY

Lanner falcon
Falco biarmicus

Widespread, but rare in low-lying bushveld. Associated with breeding cliffs, but subadult birds may wander widely. **Typical falcon appearance, rufous crown and whitish under parts** that lack conspicuous barring, streaks or spots. Peregrine Falcon *F. peregrinus* is more robustly built and lacks rufous crown. Feeds on vertebrates including birds. As in all falcons, eggs laid directly on rocky ledge on cliff. May use nests of other birds.

Length: 42 cm

Little grebe
Tachybaptus ruficollis
Occurs in suitable wetland habitats throughout the country. May be seen on almost any motionless water body including weirs, dams and seasonal pans. Identified by **small, duck-shaped body, dark plumage with rufous neck**. Forages underwater for frogs and invertebrates. Generally seen singly or in pairs, but may flock outside of the breeding season. Nest is floating mass of plant material anchored to vegetation.
Length: 20 cm

NEIL GRAY

African darter
Anhinga rufa
Occurs sparsely throughout the country. Associated with quiet, slow flowing water on dams, weirs and larger rivers. **Body plumage is dark, neck rufous**. Distinguished from cormorants by long sinuous neck and needle-sharp beak. Forages with only head and neck out of water, diving for fish and occasionally frogs. Nests colonially in heronries. Nest is a messy platform of sticks, typically built in dead tree over water.
Length: 79 cm

GERHARD GELDENHUYS

Reed cormorant
Phalacrocorax africanus
Widespread in suitable habitat. Prefers slow-moving water bodies including dams, weirs and larger rivers. **Typical cormorant-shape with long neck and beak.** Distinguished from next species by **smaller size, dark under parts and red eye**. May be seen singly or in small groups when foraging, but gregarious at roosting and nesting sites. Catches fish by diving. Nests in association with other waterbirds, usually in dead tree over water.
Length: 60 cm

GERHARD GELDENHUYS

White-breasted cormorant
Phalacrocorax lucidus
Occurs sparsely in suitable habitat throughout the country. Associated with big water bodies such as dams and larger rivers. **Typical cormorant-shape with long neck and beak.** Distinguished from previous species by **larger size, white breast and green eye**. Usually seen singly or pairs. Roosts in small groups. Catches fish by diving. Nests in heronries or in single-species groups. Nest may be in dead tree or on cliff face low over water.
Length: 90 cm

NEIL GRAY

PHIL PERRY

Little egret
Egretta garzetta
Occurs in suitable wetlands in the bushveld regions. Generally associated with the shallow shores of water bodies. Identified by **all-white plumage, long white crest, black beak and yellow feet**. Usually forages singly wading through shallow water in search of fish which it captures with its long sharp beak. Nests in heronries, usually dead tree over water.

Length: 64 cm

PHIL PERRY

Great egret
Egretta alba
Occurs sparsely in suitable wetlands in the bushveld regions. Prefers quiet, back waters on dams or marshes. Identified by **all-white plumage, very long neck and all-black legs and feet**. Beak is yellow, but turns black during breeding. Yellow-billed egret *E. intermedia* is smaller with yellowish upper legs. Usually forages singly for fish by standing motionless in relatively deep water. Nests in heronries, in dead tree over water.
Length: 95 cm

PHIL PERRY

Grey heron
Ardea cinerea, Gilonki
Occurs in suitable habitat in the bushveld regions. Seen at or near shallow water bodies including rivers and open shoreline of dams. A **large, grey-and-white bird with long neck and beak**. Distinguished from next species by **white neck and breast, pale beak and black line through eye**. Forages singly wading in shallow water in search of fish. May stand motionless for long periods. Nests in heronries, in dead tree over water.
Length: 97 cm

PHIL PERRY

W

Black-headed heron
Ardea melanocephala, Gilonki
Occurs in suitable habitat throughout the country. Associated with open, often flooded, grassland habitats. May wander some distance from closest body of water. A large, dark grey bird with long neck and beak. Distinguished from previous species by **black neck and head, with white throat**. Forages singly or in pairs, walking through grassland in search of frogs, rodents and crabs. Nests in heronries, usually in dead tree over water.
Length: 100 cm

Purple heron

Ardea purpurea

Widespread in suitable habitat. Prefers dense reed-beds along dams, rivers and marshes. **Typical heron-shaped body, grey upper parts, and rufous neck, face and under parts.** Differs from goliath heron *A. goliath* by much smaller size, more slender yellowish beak and black crown. Stands among tall reeds for long periods, in search of fish and frogs. Solitary nester, builds a platform of reeds low down in dense vegetation.

Length: 89 cm

Cattle egret

Bubulcus ibis, Lilanda

Widespread in open grassy habitats, avoiding only forest interior. Rarely far from domestic livestock or wild game. Has **all-white plumage, relatively short neck and yellowish beak and legs.** Breeding birds assume an orange hue to the head, back and breast. Seen in small to large flocks. Forages on insects flushed by cattle or game. May perch on cattle, but does not eat ticks. Roosts in large numbers and nests in reed-beds.

Length: 54 cm

Green-backed heron

Butorides striata

Occurs in bushveld wetlands fringed with dense riparian vegetation. Identified by **grey-green upper parts, yellow legs and orangish stripe running from throat to belly.** Dwarf bittern *Ixobrychus sturmii* lacks the orange stripe, and is streaked black-and-white. Little bittern *I. minutus* is buffy with black wings, back and crown. Fishes from a perch overlooking the water. Nest is small platform of twigs and reeds in dense vegetation.

Length: 41 cm

Black-crowned night-heron

Nycticorax nycticorax

Occurs sparsely in suitable habitat in the bushveld regions. Associated with water bodies fringed with mature riparian vegetation including marshes, dams and rivers. Easily identified by **white under parts, grey wings, and black back and crown.** Usually seen perched in tall dense tree by day. Hunts for fish at night. Nest is flimsy platform of twigs and reeds low in bush over water.

Length: 56 cm

Immature

PHIL PERRY

Hamerkop
Scopus umbretta, Tsekwane
Occurs throughout the country. May be seen in almost any situation, but avoids dense forest interior. Generally does not stray too far from water where it nests. Unmistakable **uniform dark brown bird with conspicuous crest, and black legs and beak.** Forages in pairs, searching for frogs and fish. Protected by Swazi culture. Nest is an enormous, roofed structure with side entrance; often taken over by owls.
Length: 56 cm

(G) (W) (SB) (B) (L)

GERHARD GELDENHUYS

Hadeda ibis
Bostrychia hagedash, Lingangane
Occurs in grassland, fallow fields, savanna, forest edge and urban lawns. Identified by **brownish plumage with metallic sheen on wings, and long decurved beak.** Glossy ibis *Plegadis falcinellus* is more slender and darker. Forages in small groups, but may roost in large flocks. Uses beak to probe in soft soil for insects. Very noisy uttering a loud "ha-ha-haheehaa". Nest is flimsy platform on horizontal fork of tree, near water.
Length: 76 cm

(G) (W) (SB) (B) (L)

GEOFF McILLERON, FIREFLY IMAGES

Southern bald ibis
Geronticus calvus, Inkondla
Occurs sparsely in the montane grassland regions. Associated with good quality grasslands, preferring short, recently burnt areas. Identified by **metallic dark green plumage, bald white neck, and red crown and beak.** At a distance appears as a dark bird with a red beak. Nests regularly at two traditional sites in Swaziland, one at Malolotja Nature Reserve. Nest is built on cliff ledge over water. "Vulnerable" in Swazi RDB.
Length: 79 cm

(G)

PHIL PERRY

African sacred ibis
Threskiornis aethiopicus
Occurs sparsely in suitable habitat throughout the country. Associated with moist habitats such as marshes, dams, rank grassland and irrigated fields. Easily identified by **white plumage with long decurved beak.** Neck, head and beak are black. Forages in small flocks by probing in soft soil. Nests colonial often with other waterbird species in mixed heronries. Nesting tree usually overhangs water.
Length: 89 cm

(W)

African spoonbill

Platalea alba

Occurs sparsely in suitable habitat throughout the bushveld regions, and rarely in montane grasslands. Associated with wetlands that have open shorelines and shallow water. Easily identified by **stork-like white body, red legs and bizarre spoon-shaped beak**. Forages by wading in shallow water, sweeping from side to side with beak half open. Breeds colonially. Nest is flat platform of twigs and sticks placed in tree or reeds.

Length: 91 cm

Yellow-billed stork

Mycteria ibis, Incecelegu

Occurs sparsely in the bushveld regions. Usually seen on open shore of dam or large river. Easily identified by **white plumage, black wings, red legs and yellow beak**. Black stork *Ciconia nigra* has black plumage, white belly and red beak. Feeds on fish, frogs and aquatic insects by wading in shallow water. Nests colonially in trees close to water, but breeding has not yet been observed in the country. "Near Threatened" in Swazi RDB.

Length: 97 cm

White stork

Ciconia ciconia, Incecelegu

Widespread as a non-breeding migrant. May be seen in any open situation including grassland, fields and open savanna. Avoids forest and dense woodland. Identified by **white under parts, neck and head, black wings and back, and red legs and beak**. Woolly-necked stork *Ciconia episcopus* has white neck, rich-brown upper parts and breast. Gregarious, forming large flocks prior to return migration. A few birds may over-winter.

Length: 120 cm

Marabou stork

Leptoptilos crumeniferus, Umcalandlovu

Occurs very sparsely in the eastern bushveld regions, mostly in Hlane National Park and around Big Bend. Associated with a variety of savanna habitats, often near water. Identified by **large size, black upper parts, whitish under parts, bare pinkish neck with gular pouch and heavy beak**. At Hlane, nests in flat-topped *Acacia tortilis*. This is the only regular breeding colony south of the Limpopo River. "Vulnerable" in Swazi RDB.

Length: 152 cm

GINA JC WILGENBUS

SB · B · F · L

Black-headed oriole
Oriolus larvatus, Kipiloni/Likiploshi
Occurs throughout the country. Associated with a wide range of wooded habitats including woodland, savanna, forest, gardens and edges of alien plantations. Easily identified by **bright yellow plumage with black head and neck, and red beak**. Gives a loud bubbling "kleeeu". Conspicuous and visible, often seen in pairs at fruiting tree. Nest is placed high up in tall leafy tree, and well concealed with moss.
Length: 25 cm

PHIL PERRY

SB · B · L

Fork-tailed drongo
Dicrurus adsimilis, Intsengu
Abundant in a wide variety of wooded habitats including savanna, woodland and forest edge. Avoids open treeless grasslands. Identified by **jet-black plumage, forked tail and reddish eye**. Similar square-tailed drongo *D. ludwigii* has square tail and inhabits forest. Highly territorial, and usually seen in pairs. Feeds predominantly on insects. Fearless, often chasing raptors. Nest is high up in horizontal fork of tall tree.
Length: 25 cm

MARK D ANDERSON

SB · B · F · L

African paradise-flycatcher
Terpsiphone viridis, Tjwatjwati
Widespread as an intra-African breeding migrant. Seen in almost any wooded habitat, avoiding only open treeless grasslands. Easily identified by **chestnut wings and tail, bluish-grey upper and under parts, white belly, and blue beak and eye-ring**. Male has much longer tail than female. Breeds throughout summer, building a neat tight cup in fork of tree. Some birds over-winter in riparian forest at lower altitudes.
Length: 18 cm

MARK D ANDERSON

B

Brubru
Nilaus afer
Occurs widely in the eastern parts of the bushveld regions. Closely associated with *Acacia nigrescens* woodland; far rarer in broadleaved woodland and scrubby savanna. Identified by **black-and-white upper parts, black crown and white under parts**. Distinguished from next species by **broken rufous stripe** along side. Call is a high pitched trill reminiscent of the ring of a telephone. Nest is well concealed in tall tree.
Length: 14 cm

Black-backed puffback
Dryoscopus cubla
Occurs throughout the country in almost any wooded situation including woodland, savanna, gardens, forest and forest edge. Identified by **black upper parts, white under parts, white rump and red eye**. Male has black crown extending over eye; female has white eye stripe. Conspicuous and highly vocal during the breeding season. Tidy nest built by female in high vertical fork of tree, accompanied by calling male.
Length: 17 cm

Black-crowned tchagra
Tchagra senegalus, Umngumphane
Occurs widely in the country, but absent from the highest altitudes in the west. Associated with a variety of wooded habitats ranging from forest edge to open savanna. Identified by **light brown upper parts, pale under parts, rufous wing and white eye stripe**. Distinguished from next species by **black crown**. A territorial species usually seen in pairs. Nest is characteristically placed low in vertical fork of shrub.
Length: 22 cm

Brown-crowned tchagra
Tchagra australis
Occurs throughout the bushveld regions. Associated with woodland and savanna habitats; more common in *Acacia* savanna than broad-leaved woodland. Similar to previous species from which it is distinguished by **brown crown**. Male performs an aerial display, rising above the canopy followed by gliding descent with fanned tail uttering double-noted "da-ru, da-ru, da-ru". Nest placed low in vertical fork of shrub.
Length: 20 cm

Southern boubou
Laniarius ferrugineus
Occurs widely throughout the country. Associated with dense vegetation and tangles, including forest, forest edge and bush-encroached savanna. Avoids open habitats. Identified by **black upper parts, white wing bar, creamish under parts darkening to a rufous vent**. Best located by highly variable duet call. Skulking and often difficult to see clearly. Nest is well hidden in low thicket.
Length: 22 cm

75

Bokmakierie
Telophorus zeylonus
Occurs in the montane grassland region where it is closely associated with rocky outcrops interspersed in shrub woodland. Identified by **olive-green upper parts, grey head, yellow under parts** with a conspicuous **black breast band**. Usually seen in pairs, concealed in thicket. However, can readily be located by loud duet. Nest is built low in dense thicket.

Length: 23 cm

Orange-breasted bush-shrike
Telophorus sulfureopectus
Occurs throughout the bushveld regions. Usually seen in a variety of wooded habitats, only avoiding montane grasslands. Identified by **olive-green upper parts, grey head and orange breast**. Distinguished from next species by more **slender beak** and indistinct **yellow eye stripe**. Olive bush-shrike *T. olivaceus* has uniform yellow or cream under parts and is restricted to forest. Nest is flimsy platform in short thorny tree.
Length: 19 cm

Gorgeous bush-shrike
Telophorus viridis
Occurs widely in the bushveld regions. Closely associated with thickets and dense tangles particularly along rivers, avoiding more open situations. Identified by **olive-green upper parts and head, yellow under parts, black breast band enclosing brilliant red throat**. Best located by call, a loud "kong-kowit-kowit". Very skulking and difficult to observe, but may respond to spishing. Nest is placed low down in thicket.
Length: 19 cm

Grey-headed bush-shrike
Malaconotus blanchoti
Occurs throughout the bushveld regions. Associated with a variety of wooded habitats. Identified by **olive-green upper parts, grey head and orange breast**. Distinguished from previous species by more **robust beak**. Usually seen in pairs. Male and female maintain contact through a variety of calls. May move to higher altitudes during dry winter months following drought. Nest is a platform of twigs placed high up in tall tree.
Length: 26 cm

White-crested helmet-shrike
Prionops plumatus, Umtimbakazane
Occurs widely in bushveld. Associated with a variety of woodland habitats, but highest densities in broadleaved woodland. Identified by **black-and-white upper parts, white under parts, red legs and yellow eye-ring**. Retz's helmet-shrike *P. retzii* has dark brown plumage and red legs and beak. Lives in small groups which cooperate to assist alpha male and female raise offspring. Nest is tidy cup placed in fork of tree.
Length: 19 cm

Cape batis
Batis capensis
Restricted to forest patches in montane grasslands and Lebombos. Occurs in montane and scarp forests, and exotic plantations. Identified by **small size, green-brown upper parts, white under parts, grey head and black mask**. Breast band is black in male and rufous in female. Distinguished from next species by **rufous flanks and rufous wing spots**. Usually seen in pairs. Nest is small tidy cup placed low in vegetation.
Length: 12 cm

Chinspot batis
Batis molitor, Incwincwi
Occurs widely in the bushveld regions. Associated with savanna and woodland; highest densities in *Acacia* savanna. Similar in size and behaviour to the previous species from which it can be distinguished by **white flanks and white wing spots**. Breast band is black in male and rufous in female. Very confiding and will approach observer who is spishing. Nest is small cup placed in lower branches of tree.
Length: 12 cm

Pied crow
Corvus albus, Lihubhulu
Occurs in almost any habitat except forest. Generally most abundant where associated with humans. Identified by **jet black plumage, and white breast and neck**. The smaller-sized Cape crow *C. capensis* has no white markings. Usually seen in small groups. Forages on the ground feeding on fruits and insects. Also takes carrion and regularly frequents dump sites. Large nest is placed in fork of tree or on man-made structure.
Length: 49 cm

77

PHIL PERRY

White-necked raven
Corvus albicollis, Lihwabayi
Occurs in mountainous terrain to the west and Lebombos to the east of the country. Mostly absent from the bushveld regions. Easily identified by **large size, jet black plumage and white neck**. Distinguished from previous species by larger size and lack of white on the breast. Usually seen in pairs. Nest is large mass of twigs and sticks, placed on cliff face.

G   L

Length: 52 cm

PHIL PERRY

Red-backed shrike
Lanius collurio
Occurs as a non-breeding migrant throughout the bushveld regions. Highest densities in *Acacia* savanna, but also present in other woodland habitats. Identified by **rufous back, grey head and dark mask**. Under parts white in the male and lightly barred in the female. Male perches prominently on top of bush, while female is less conspicuous remaining more concealed within bush. Birds are present between November and April.
Length: 18 cm

SB   B   L

PHIL PERRY

Common fiscal
Lanius collaris, Lilunga
Widespread but absent from the eastern bushveld. Prefers lightly wooded habitats, especially grasslands interspersed with a few trees. Identified by **black upper parts, with a white "V" on the back, and white under parts**. Female is duller than the male. Distinguished from southern boubou *Laniarius ferrugineus* by posture and behaviour. Often perches prominently on top of bush or tree. Bulky nest is often situated in thorny bush.
Length: 22 cm

G   SB   L

MARK D ANDERSON

Magpie shrike
Corvinella melanoleuca
Occurs only in the extreme eastern parts of the bushveld regions. Associated with open *Acacia nigrescens* savanna, avoiding dense woodland and bush-encroached thicket. Easily identified by **black plumage, white wing markings and very long tail**. Observed in small groups where members assist alpha male and female to raise offspring. Nest is bulky cup of grass, twigs and roots.
Length: 45 cm

B

Black cuckooshrike
Campephaga flava
Widespread and associated with wooded habitats; highest densities in broadleaved woodland, but also in *Acacia* savanna and riparian forest. Male is **uniform jet black**. Distinguished from other all-black birds by **yellow gape**. Yellow shoulder patch is occasionally present. Female has mottled yellow-brown upper parts and barred yellow-brown under parts. Nest is barely visible shallow cup of moss and lichen in canopy of tall tree.
Length: 21 cm

SB B L

Southern black tit
Parus niger
Occurs throughout the country in a variety of wooded habitats. Avoids open grasslands. Identified by **black plumage with white wings**. May be seen in pairs or small family groups that defend a territory against other pairs. Forages for insects which it plucks off branches and under bark. Some of the groups have extra birds that assist the alpha pair with raising offspring. Eggs are laid in natural tree cavity.
Length: 15 cm

SB B F L

Brown-throated martin
Riparia paludicola
Widely but patchily distributed and generally rare in the eastern bushveld regions. Most frequently seen in montane grasslands. Prefers open situations near water, especially rivers. Identified by uniform **dark brown upper parts, and whitish belly** which contrasts with dark throat and breast. Usually seen in small flocks near nesting sites. Breeds colonially in tunnels dug into the side of earth banks, often river cuttings.
Length: 13 cm

G W

Banded martin
Riparia cincta, Inkonjane
An intra-African migrant restricted to montane grassland. Prefers open grasslands near small mountain streams. Identified by **dark brown upper parts, white under parts and a brown breast band**. White eye stripe can be seen at close range. Differs from sand martin *R. riparia* by **white under wing coverts and eye stripe**. Pairs often fly low over grassland foraging for insects. Nest is at end of tunnel in earth bank.
Length: 18 cm

G W

PHIL PERRY

G SB B L

Barn swallow
Hirundo rustica, Inkonjane
Can be seen anywhere in the country where it occurs as a non-breeding migrant. Identified by **dark upper parts, whitish under parts with black band** enclosing a **rufous throat**. Distinguished from the next species by lack of white throat. May be seen in small to very large flocks between October and April. Gathers by the hundreds on telephone lines before the return migration. Roosts communally in reed-beds.
Length: 20 cm

MARK D ANDERSON

G W

White-throated swallow
Hirundo albigularis, Inkonjane
Occurs as an intra-African migrant in the montane grassland region. Associated with moist grasslands and vleis, often near water. Similar to previous species from which it can be distinguished by its **white throat**. Under parts are white with black breast band. Seen singly or in pairs. Nest is a half-cup made with mud attached under overhang of rock face or man-made structure such as a bridge.
Length: 15 cm

GEOFF McILLERON, FIREFLY IMAGES

W

Wire-tailed swallow
Hirundo smithii, Inkonjane
Widespread in suitable habitat, but mostly absent from western montane grasslands. Associated with rivers and larger streams. Identified by **white under parts, dark blue upper parts, rufous crown, and very long thin outer tail feathers**. Grey-rumped swallow *Pseudhirundo griseopyga* has grey head and pale grey rump. Seen singly or in pairs; often perches on bridges. Nest is a mud half-cup, often attached under overhang of bridge.
Length: 17 cm

GEOFF McILLERON, FIREFLY IMAGES

G

Blue swallow
Hirundo atrocaerulea, Inkonjane
Intra-African migrant, regularly seen only at Malolotja Nature Reserve. Associated with montane grasslands. Identified by uniform **metallic dark blue plumage**. Told from the black saw-wing (below) by plumage colour and **very long thin outer tail feathers**. Present October to April. Nest is half-cup of mud and grass stuck to roof of antbear *Orycterops afer* burrow. "Critically Endangered" in the Swazi RDB, due to extensive habitat loss.
Length: 22 cm

Greater striped swallow
Hirundo cucullata, Inkonjane

Intra-African migrant to the western montane grasslands. Prefers open grasslands, but may also be seen flying over wooded habitats. Has **dark upper parts, lightly streaked whitish under parts, rufous crown and rump**. Distinguished from the next species by **white ear patch, lighter streaking, paler rump and call**. Present September to May. Nest is mud bowl with tunnel entrance stuck on rock face, bridge or building.
Length: 19 cm

Lesser striped swallow
Hirundo abyssinica, Inkonjane

Widespread intra-Africa mirant, absent only from the extreme west. Associated with wooded habitats. Has **dark upper parts, boldly streaked whitish under parts, rufous crown and rump**. Distinguished from previous species by **rufous ear patch, bold streaking, darker rump and call**. Present August to May. Nest is mud bowl with tunnel entrance stuck on rock face, bridge or building, often re-used in successive years.
Length: 17 cm

Red-breasted swallow
Hirundo semirufa

Occurs as an intra-African migrant in suitable habitat in the bushveld regions. Usually seen in savanna close to nest site. Identified by **dark upper parts, rufous under parts and rump**. Distinguished from previous two species by lack of white under parts. Present between September and April. Forages singly or in pairs. Nest is mud bowl with tunnel entrance, generally attached to roof of road culvert.
Length: 24 cm

Rock martin
Hirundo fuligula, Inkonjane

Occurs in suitable habitat in the mountainous west and Lebombos in the east of the country. Absent from most of the bushveld regions. Closely associated with cliffs either in open grassland or in savanna. Identified by **plain brown plumage** with characteristic **white windows visible in the tail** at close range. Usually seen in pairs near breeding cliffs. Nest is half-cup of mud attached under overhang of rock.
Length: 15 cm

81

NICO MYBURGH

G SB

Black saw-wing
Psalidoprocne holomelaena, Inkonjane
Occurs widely in the western half of the country. May be seen in a variety of habitats including montane grassland and savanna, but most frequently in the forest/grassland ecotone. Identified by **jet-black plumage**. Distinguished from the blue swallow (above) by **darker plumage and relatively short outer tail feathers**. Seen singly, in pairs or small groups. Nest is at the end of a tunnel in earth bank.
Length: 17 cm

PHIL PERRY

G SB B F L

Dark-capped bulbul
Pycnonotus tricolor, Ligoholo/Ligibholo
Very common and widespread bird occurring in almost all habitats except treeless grasslands. Identified by **brown upper and under parts, yellow vent, dark face and modest crest**. Lively and noisy bird that may be seen singly, in pairs or in flocks. Feeds on fruit and insects. Confiding most of the time, but secretive around the nest which is typically constructed of fine plant material and placed high up in tall, leafy tree.
Length: 21 cm

PHIL PERRY

F SB L

Sombre greenbul
Andropadus importunus, Umgwalane
Widespread but rare in the extreme west. Prefers dense vegetation including forest, forest edge and closed woodland. Absent from grasslands and open savanna. Identified by uniform **olive-green plumage** with conspicuous **pale eye** visible at close range. Best located by call "Willie, puty-puty-puty, pheoee". Skulks in thickets, rarely coming out into the open. Nest is thin cup of fine plant material, often low down in bush.
Length: 21 cm

LEX HES

F SB L

Terrestrial brownbul
Phyllastrephus terrestris
Occurs in the bushveld. Associated with dense vegetation, especially riparian forest. Identified by **rich-brown upper parts, paler under parts, white throat** contrasting with **greyish breast and red eye**. Best located by call which is a series of harsh chattering notes. Lives in small groups; members not straying far from each other. Moves along forest floor searching for insects. Nest made of fine plant material, typically low down in bush.
Length: 22 cm

Eastern nicator

Nicator gularis

Occurs throughout the bushveld regions. Closely associated with dense vegetation, especially riparian forest. Identified by **olive-green upper parts, paler under parts, yellow vent** and conspicuous **white wing spots**. Skulking and difficult to observe well, but easily located by call which is similar but more musical than previous species. Nest is made of fine plant material, typically low down in bush.

Length: 23 cm

Cape grassbird

Sphenoeacus afer

Occurs widely in montane grassland, the western bushveld and the highest parts of the Lebombos. Associated with rank grasslands, near a stream or other water body. Has **rufous head, wings and rump, mottled black-and-brown back and creamish under parts**. Resembles a cisticola, but much larger. Can be confiding, but usually located by call. Lives singly or in pairs. Nest is untidy mass of grass, placed in dense grass.

Length: 21 cm

Long-billed crombec

Sylvietta rufescens

Occurs widely in the bushveld regions. Associated with savannas and woodlands, but highest densities in *Acacia* savanna. Identified by **grey upper parts, pale orange under parts and very short tail** giving it the appearance of lacking a tail. An active and vocal bird that is often seen in mixed bird parties. Nest is unusual roofed structure made of spider web and plant material that hangs down from a low branch of a bush.

Length: 11 cm

Burnt-necked eremomela

Eremomela usticollis

Occurs sparsely in the extreme eastern parts of the bushveld region. Closely associated with *Acacia* savanna, particularly short scrubby habitats. Identified by **grey upper parts, pale orangish-cream under parts** with inconspicuous **rufous bar across throat, and pale eye**. The Yellow-bellied eremomela *E. icteropygialis* lacks the throat bar and has a yellow belly and vent. Encountered in pairs or small flocks.

Length: 10 cm

W

Little rush-warbler
Bradypterus baboecala
Occurs widely in suitable habitat throughout the country. Closely associated with reed-beds, sedges and bulrushes. Has **rich brown upper parts, paler under parts, with short rounded wings and tail**. Best identified by call as series of "krak" notes that speed up to a trill. Skulking and rarely seen in the open, but may respond to spishing. Nest is placed low down in sedge or bulrush plant.
Length: 17 cm

W

African reed-warbler
Acrocephalus baeticatus
Occurs widely as an intra-African migrant in suitable habitat. Closely associated with reed-beds. Not easily identified in the field due to skulking nature, but may be distinguished from the marsh warbler *A. palustris* by relatively **shorter wings, habitat and call**. The marsh warbler rarely enters reed-beds, instead calls incessantly in late summer from dense vegetation near water. Nest is neat cup of grass attached to stem of reeds.
Length: 13 cm

W

Lesser swamp-warbler
Acrocephalus gracilirostris
Occurs in suitable habitat throughout the country. Closely associated with reed-beds, which it rarely leaves. Difficult to identify in the field due to skulking behaviour, but **larger** than the previous species, with an inconspicuous **white eye stripe and rufous flanks**. Much smaller than the similar great reed-warbler *A. arundinaceus*. Rarely seen, but calls frequently especially in summer. Nest is attached to stem of reed.
Length: 17 cm

G   W

Dark-capped yellow warbler
Chloropeta natalensis
Occurs widely in suitable habitat in montane grassland; scarce in the eastern parts of the country. Closely associated with rank vegetation, especially tall moist grass near stream or marsh. Easily identified when seen by **olive-green upper parts, and bright yellow under parts**. Generally difficult to see, but may be called up by spishing. Forages singly or in pairs. Nest is attached to the stem of an herbaceous plant.
Length: 14 cm

WILL NICHOL

MARK D ANDERSON

GEOFF MCILLERON, FIREFLY IMAGES

PETER GINN

Willow warbler
Phylloscopus trochilus
Common non-breeding migrant seen from October to April in a variety of wooded habitats, but highest densities in broadleaved woodland. A variable species; **upper parts olive-green to grey-brown, under parts generally pale cream** occasionally washed pale yellow. Differs from icterine warbler *Hippolais icterina* by **dull-reddish, not black, legs**. An active bird that flits through the mid- and upper canopy in search of insects.
Length: 11 cm

Arrow-marked babbler
Turdoides jardineii
Occurs throughout the bushveld regions. Associated with a range of savanna and woodland habitats. Identified by **grey-brown plumage, finely speckled with white spots, and red eye**. Lives in small family groups, member of which assist alpha pair to raise offspring. Call is very loud and grating "kra-kra-kra-kra", and actively mobs predators. Nest is untidy cup of plant material, usually well concealed in low fork of tree.
Length: 24 cm

Cape white-eye
Zosterops virens, Mehlwane
Occurs widely in the country, but scarce in the extreme east of the bushveld region. Associated with a wide range of wooded habitats including forest, forest edge, gardens, dense woodland and exotic plantations. Easily identified by **small size, olive-green upper parts, yellowish under parts, and white eye-ring**. Forages in pairs or small flocks, feeding on insects and fruit. Nest is thin cup of grass placed low down in thicket.
Length: 12 cm

Rattling cisticola
Cisticola chiniana
Very common in the bushveld. Prefers savanna habitats including woodland, thornveld, bush-encroached thicket, degraded bush and fallow fields. Has **rufous upper parts faintly streaked black, and pale under parts**. Similar wailing cisticola *C. lais* restricted to montane grassland. Best identified by call "tsip-tsip-tsip-tsip-treeoooee" often given from prominent perch. Dome-shaped grass nest is placed at the base of shrub in dense grass.
Length: 15 cm

MARK D ANDERSON

Levaillant's cisticola
Cisticola tinniens
Occurs in montane grassland and the extreme western parts of the bushveld regions. Associated with rank vegetation near streams and marshes, including bulrushes and sedges. Identified by **rufous upper parts boldly streaked black, and pale under parts**. Seen in pairs or small family groups. Forages low down in vegetation, flying up to higher perch when disturbed. Nest is domed ball of grass placed low in herbaceous plant.
Length: 13 cm

HUGH CHITTENDEN

Croaking cisticola
Cisticola natalensis
Occurs widely but patchily. Associated with open grassy areas near water; most abundant in montane grassland, and absent from dense woodland. Distinguished from all other cisticolas by more **robust build, heavy beak, and lack of rufous wash to upper parts or head**. Highly visible and vocal in the breeding season when it calls from prominent perch or in flight. Nest is domed ball of grass placed at base of grass tuft.
Length: 16 cm

MARK D ANDERSON

Neddicky
Cisticola fulvicapilla
Occurs throughout except in the extreme eastern parts of the bushveld region. Usually seen in hilly broken terrain with scattered trees or rocky outcrops. Avoids densely wooded situations. Identified by **plain rufous upper parts and head without any streaking, and pale under parts**. Distinguished from similar lazy cisticola *C. aberrans* by short tail. Nest is domed ball of grass placed at base of shrub in dense grass.
Length: 11 cm

PETER GINN

Zitting cisticola
Cisticola juncidis, Ncedze
Occurs widely. Usually seen in open situations including montane grassland, clearings and fields in the bushveld region, and marshes. Identified by **small size and short tail. Upper parts washed rufous with black streaks, and pale under parts**. Best distinguished from similar desert cisticola *C. aridulus* by call "zit-zit-zit" uttered without wing-snap. Nest is domed mass of grass with top entrance, placed low in dense grass.
Length: 11 cm

Wing-snapping cisticola

Cisticola ayresii

Restricted to montane grasslands, in open areas covered with short grass. A small cisticola with **upper parts washed rufous with black streaks, and pale under parts**. Best distinguished from previous species by **call** "chitik-pee-pee-pee" uttered high in the sky, descends with audible wing snaps. Similar desert cisticola *C. aridulus* is absent from montane grasslands. Nest is dome-shaped ball of grass placed at base of grass tuft.

Length: 10 cm

Tawny-flanked prinia

Prinia subflava

Widespread in a variety of habitats but generally in rank vegetation close to water. Identified by **uniform brown upper parts, creamish under parts** with conspicuous **light rufous wash to flanks, and flesh-coloured legs**. Drakensberg prinia *P. hypoxantha* has yellowish under parts streaked black. The long tail is often cocked. Seen in pairs or small family groups. Domed nest with side entrance woven into a low shrub or tall herb.

Length: 13 cm

Bar-throated apalis

Apalis thoracica

Occurs in montane grassland and the highest parts of the Lebombo Mountains in densely wooded habitats. Identified by **olive-green upper parts, pale under parts washed with light yellow on belly**, and conspicuous **black breast band**. Distinguished from similar Rudd's apalis *A. ruddi* by pale eye and habitat. Confiding and responds to spishing. Nest is oval-shaped with side entrance concealed in thicket.

Length: 12 cm

Yellow-breasted apalis

Apalis flavida

Occurs widely in the bushveld. Associated with a variety of wooded habitats including savanna, woodland, riparian forest and forest edge. Easily identified by **olive-green upper parts, grey head, yellow breast and red eye**. Male has small black blotch at base of yellow breast. Seen in pairs or small family groups. Confiding and responds to spishing. Messy oval nest with side entrance placed in the canopy of a thorn tree.

Length: 12 cm

87

LEX HES

Green-backed camaroptera
Camaroptera brachyura
Widespread preferring dense tangled vegetation, but also seen in exotic plantations, forest edge and gardens. Identified by **olive-green upper parts, greyish under parts and head, and reddish eye**. Short tail is often flicked up and down. Best located by **call**, a loud plaintive "kwik, kwik, kwik" uttered from concealed situation. Responds to spishing. Nest is untidy mass of leaves woven together and placed low in shrub or bush.
Length: 12 cm

MARK D ANDERSON

Rufous-naped lark
Mirafra africana, Sangole
Occurs throughout the country. Encountered in a variety of open habitats including grassland, fields, and clearings in savanna. Generally prefers short, heavily grazed grassland. Identified by **rufous crest and wings, light brown streaked upper parts and pale under parts**. Best distinguished by **call** a loud whistle "tree-trieu" usually given from the top of a short bush or ant hill. Nest is placed at the base of a grass tuft.
Length: 17 cm

MARK D ANDERSON

B

Sabota lark
Calendulauda sabota
Restricted to the eastern bushveld where it is more abundant in the south than the north. Seen in lightly wooded *Acacia* savanna, absent from dense woodland. Identified by **streaked upper parts, whitish under parts with streaking on breast**, and conspicuous **white eye stripe**. Forages on ground, but sings from top of a bush or tree. Nest is grass cup on the ground. Nestlings leave nest well before they are able to fly.
Length: 15 cm

GERHARD GELDENHUYS

G L

Cape rock-thrush
Monticola rupestris
Occurs in mountainous terrain in western montane grassland and the Lebombos in the east. Seen in boulder-strewn habitats in open grassland or savanna. Has conspicuous **blue-grey head and neck, orange body with streaked upper parts**. Differs from sentinel rock-thrush *M. explorator* by lack of blue-grey upper parts. Often sits on prominent perch. Nest is large messy collection of twigs, grass and roots wedged between rocks.
Length: 22 cm

Groundscraper thrush

Psophocichla litsitsirupa, Incuphabulongo
Occurs in suitable habitat throughout the country. Typically encountered in open habitats with short grass or bare ground including grasslands, cultivated fields, lawns and savanna. Identified by **grey-brown upper parts and boldly streaked under parts**. Forages singly or in pairs on the ground in search of insects. Confiding and easy to observe. Nest is bulky mass of plant material placed in main fork of tall tree.
Length: 22 cm

PHIL PERRY

G   SB   B   L

Kurrichane thrush

Turdus libonyanus, Incuphabulongo/Gawozi
Common and widespread throughout the country. Associated with lightly wooded habitats, avoiding forest interior and treeless grasslands. Identified by **brown upper parts, pale under parts, rufous flanks, black malar stripe and orange beak**. Similar olive thrush *T. olivaceus* is restricted to montane forest and has entire belly orange, with yellowish beak. Nest is untidy mass of grass and roots concealed in main fork of large tree.
Length: 21 cm

NEIL GRAY

G   SB   B   L

Pale flycatcher

Bradornis pallidus
Occurs throughout the bushveld regions. Associated with *Acacia* savanna, much more scarce in broadleaved savanna. Identified by plain light brown upper parts with slightly paler under parts, and the lack of any conspicuous markings. A quiet bird that is easily overlooked, but is confiding and responds to spishing. Seen in pairs. Nest is neat delicate cup placed in fork of short scrubby tree.
Length: 16 cm

NEIL GRAY

SB   B   L

Southern black flycatcher

Melaenornis pammelaina, Mantsengwane
Widespread in wooded habitats. May be seen in savanna, woodland, forest edge, gardens and exotic plantations. Identified by **all black plumage and square tail**. The similar square-tailed drongo *Dicrurus ludwigii* inhabits forests and is a noisy bird of the canopy. A quiet, inquisitive bird that forages in pairs or small family groups. Nest is typically delicate cup of thin twigs and grass concealed in top of tree stump or cavity.
Length: 21 cm

MARK D ANDERSON

SB   B   F   L

MIKE UNWIN

F

African dusky flycatcher
Muscicapa adusta

Widespread breeding resident in wooded habitats in the west; non-breeding winter visitor in the east. Seen in montane forest, forest edge, gardens and exotic plantations. Restricted to riparian forest in the east. Identified by **dumpy build, dark upper parts, paler under parts lightly streaked black**. Differs from spotted flycatcher *M. striata* in **darker plumage, habitat and call**. Nest is neat tight cup in tree cavity, building or rock.
Length: 13 cm

LEX HES

F

Ashy flycatcher
Muscicapa caerulescens

Occurs sparsely in the bushveld regions. Closely tied to forest and forest edge habitats, particularly riparian forest. Identified by **uniform blue-grey plumage and lack of any conspicuous markings**. Similar grey tit-flycatcher *Myioparus plumbeus* has more slender build and conspicuous white outer tail feathers. Seen singly or in pairs. Easily overlooked due to quiet nature, but responds to spishing. Nest is neat cup in tree cavity.
Length: 15 cm

MARK D ANDERSON

F   SB

Cape robin-chat
Cossypha caffra

Widespread resident in suitable habitat in montane grassland region; non-breeding winter visitor to lower altitudes including Lebombos. Associated with a variety of wooded habitats. Identified by **brown upper parts, orange throat and breast, contrasting white belly, rufous rump and white eye stripe**. Generally skulking but responds to spishing. Nest untidy collection of plant material placed on ground in thicket.
Length: 17 cm

MIKE UNWIN

F   SB   L

White-browed robin-chat
Cossypha heuglini

Occurs widely throughout the bushveld regions. Closely associated with densely vegetated habitats including riparian forest, forest edge, gardens and dense woodland. Has **orange under parts, greyish wings, black head with conspicuous white eye stripe**. White-throated robin-chat *C. humeralis* is smaller with white throat, breast and belly. Very vocal, calling frequency at dawn and dusk. Untidy nest is placed on ground in thicket.
Length: 20 cm

Red-capped robin-chat
Cossypha natalensis
Sparsely distributed in the bushveld regions. More restricted to forest than previous species, including scarp forest and mature riparian forest. Identified by **orange under parts, grey wings and dirty brown cap** contrasting with **orange face and throat**. Differs from next species in lack of black head and upper parts. Difficult to see due to skulking habit, remaining concealed in thick tangles. Nest is placed on ground in thicket.
Length: 18 cm

NEIL GRAY

Chorister robin-chat
Cossypha dichroa
Restricted to suitable habitat in the montane grassland region. Associated with montane forest, forest edge, gardens and exotic plantations. Has **orange under parts, black head and upper parts**. Previous species has grey wings, orange face with dirty brown cap. Skulking and difficult to observe, keeping to dense vegetation, but highly vocal in summer. Easily overlooked in winter. Nest is placed on ground in thicket.
Length: 19 cm

GEOFF McILLERON, FIREFLY IMAGES

White-browed scrub-robin
Cercotrichas leucophrys, Umtjelele
Occurs throughout the bushveld regions. May be encountered in a variety of savanna habitats. Identified by **brown upper parts, white spots on wings, heavily streaked under parts and white eye stripe**. The bearded scrub-robin *C. quadrivirgata* has black malar stripe and rufous flanks. Very abundant bird, but easily overlooked when not calling. Nest is untidy mass of grass, placed at base of thorny shrub.
Length: 15 cm

PETER GINN

African stonechat
Saxicola torquatus, Indayi
Common and widespread resident in suitable habitat in montane grasslands; non-breeding winter visitor to rest of the country. Habitats include forest edge, lightly wooded grasslands, gardens, exotic plantations and clearings in savanna. Has **rufous-orange breast, white belly, black head, neck and upper parts with white shoulders and white wing bar**. Nest is untidy mass of grass placed on ground in dense grass or earth bank.
Length: 14 cm

MARK D ANDERSON

G

Buff-streaked chat
Oenanthe bifasciata
Restricted to the montane grassland region. Closely associated with rocky outcrops in grasslands above 1000 m. Male identified by **mottled brown upper parts and head, white wing bar, black throat and breast, and light orange belly**. Female is duller and lacks black throat. Seen in pairs or small family groups, perching conspicuously on rocks, drawing attention by its loud call. Nest is hidden between rocks.
Length: 17 cm

G SB L

Familiar chat
Cercomela familiaris
Occurs in mountainous terrain in the western montane grassland and Lebombos in the east. Seen in a variety of broken habitats, but never far from rocky outcrops. Has **uniform grey-brown plumage, rufous rump and light orange belly**. The larger ant-eating chat *Myrmecocichla formicivora* is uniformly dark brown with white wings. Confiding and perches singly or in pairs. Nest is placed in a niche in rock, earth bank or building.
Length: 15 cm

G L

Mocking cliff-chat
Thamnolaea cinnamomeiventris
Sparsely distributed in mountainous terrain in the montane grassland region in the west and Lebombos in the east. Favours rocky situations in wooded habitats. Male is easily identified by **jet-black upper parts, head and breast, white wing bar and rufous belly**. Female is duller and lacks wing bar. Usually seen in pairs, drawing attention by loud and penetrating call. Often takes over swallow nests.
Length: 21 cm

SB F L

Red-winged starling
Onychognathus morio, Lisomi
Widespread and common throughout the country, but rare or absent in eastern parts of the bushveld region. May be encountered in wooded broken hilly situations, but is also associated with human habitation. Male identified by **jet-black plumage and strikingly contrasting red wing**. Female has duller head. Call is loud "pheeooeee". Nest is messy collection of grass wedged in rock crevice or roof of building.
Length: 28 cm

Black-bellied starling
Lamprotornis corruscus
Sparsely distributed in suitable habitat in the east and north of the country; most abundant in the Lebombos. Prefers forest, especially riparian forest, and forest edge. Identified by **glossy metallic green upper parts, head and breast, black belly and pale eye**. The next species lacks black belly and is generally absent from forest. Seen in pairs or small groups foraging high up in canopy. Nest is situated in natural tree cavity or old barbet hole.
Length: 21 cm

VICTOR ROBERTS

Cape glossy starling
Lamprotornis nitens, Likhweti
Common and widespread throughout the bushveld. Seen in almost any habitat except treeless grasslands and forest interior. Identified by **metallic green plumage, blue-purple belly and pale eye**. The larger Burchell's starling *L. australis* has a black eye, and is restricted to the extreme eastern parts of the bushveld region. In pairs when breeding, otherwise in small flocks. Nest is placed in large tree cavity, often low in main trunk.
Length: 22 cm

GERHARD GELDENHUYS

Violet-backed starling
Cinnyricinclus leucogaster
Occurs widely as an intra-African migrant throughout the bushveld. Seen in savanna and woodland habitats; highest densities in *Acacia* savanna. Male identified by **bright iridescent violet upper parts, head and throat, and white belly**. Female is drab brown above, white below and heavily streaked throughout. Present October to April, when highly visible. Nest is placed in tree cavity, usually low down in main trunk.
Length: 18 cm

GINA JC WILGENBUS

Red-billed oxpecker
Buphagus erythrorhynchus
Common only in Hlane National Park and surrounding areas. Occurs in various savanna habitats, but always associated with large antelopes or livestock. Identified by **dark brown upper parts and throat, pale under parts, red beak and yellow eye**. Usually seen in small flocks perched on large mammalian ungulates, searching for ectoparasites including ticks. Nest is situated in tree cavity. "Near Threatened" in the Swazi RDB.
Length: 21 cm

PHIL PERRY

Amethyst sunbird

Chalcomitra amethystina, Incwincwi

Widespread but rare or absent in the eastern bush-veld. Associated with wooded habitats including forest edge, wooded grasslands and gardens. Male identified by **metallic black plumage; green cap and purple throat** only seen in good light. Female is drab brown. Gathers in small flocks at flowering plants such as aloes to feed on nectar. Nest is delicate oval mass with side entrance suspended from thin twig, often conspicuous in tree.
Length: 14 cm

Scarlet-chested sunbird

Chalcomitra senegalensis, Incwincwi

Occurs widely in the bushveld, in almost any habitat including savanna, woodland, gardens and degraded habitats. Male has **metallic black plumage and brilliant red chest; green patch on forehead and throat** only seen in good light. Female drab brown, with heavily streaked throat. Feeds on nectar, but also takes insects, especially emerging termites. Nest is messy oval structure suspended from thin outer twig of thorny tree.
Length: 14 cm

Malachite sunbird

Nectarinia famosa

Restricted to northern montane grasslands, particularly Malolotja Nature Reserve. Associated with wooded hill-slopes, especially proteas. Easily identified by **large size, very long decurved beak and elongated central tail feathers**. Male is bright metallic green, female is duller green-brown. Usually conspicuous when present, vocal and actively chasing other sunbirds. Nest is oval mass often suspended low in bush near water.
Length: 23 cm

Collared sunbird

Hedydipna collaris, Incwincwi/Intotwana

Occurs widely in the bushveld in dense wood-ed habitats including riparian forest, forest edge, bushclumps and gardens. Identified by **small size, relatively short beak for a sunbird, green upper parks and yellow under parts**. Male has green throat. Usually seen in pairs, flitting through leafy tree searching for nectar, insects and small fruit. Nest is oval mass with tangling pieces, attached to outer branch of dense tree.
Length: 11 cm

Greater double-collared sunbird

Cinnyris afer, Incwincwi

Occurs widely in montane grasslands on lightly wooded grassy slopes, also in forest edge and gardens. Male has **metallic dirty green upper parts, green throat with broad red chest band and dirty white belly**. Chest band and call differ from southern double-collared sunbird *C. chalybeus,* which is restricted to montane forest. Female is drab brown. Nest, suspended from small tree, is oval with side entrance covered by a "porch".

Length: 15 cm

White-bellied sunbird

Cinnyris talatala, Incwincwi

Common and widespread, avoiding only the highest parts of the montane grassland in the extreme west. Favours various savanna habitats, riparian forest, forest edge and gardens. Male has **metallic green upper parts, throat and chest, and white belly**. Female is drab brown with whitish under parts. Present all year round, but more abundant in winter and early summer. Nest is oval mass suspended from thorny tree, often low down.

Length: 11 cm

Marico sunbird

Cinnyris mariquensis

Occurs in the eastern bushveld in *Acacia* savanna. Has **metallic green upper parts and throat, black belly** separated from throat by **narrow reddish-purple breast band**. Purple-banded sunbird *C. bifasciatus* is smaller, with shorter beak and different call. Seen singly or in pairs, often at flowering trees and bushes. Nest is oval ball with side entrance, lined on the outside with pale bark, suspended from thin twig of tree or bush.

Length: 14 cm

Gurney's sugarbird

Promerops gurneyi

Restricted to Malolotja Nature Reserve in the montane grassland region. Associated with protea-dominated hill slopes. Easily identified by **dark brown upper parts, rufous crown and chest, white belly and yellow vent**. Tail is elongated, and beak is slightly decurved. Male defends a breeding territory, and disputes end in birds chasing each other. Nest is neat cup well concealed in foliage of tree.

Length: 27 cm

95

Spectacled weaver
Ploceus ocularis, Lihlokohloko
Occurs widely, but absent in the extreme west. Prefers wooded habitats including riparian forest, forest edge, dense woodland and gardens. Identified by **greenish upper parts, yellow under parts, and black line from beak through the eye**. Male has black throat. Unlike most weavers, lives in pairs feeding on insects and fruit. Nest is tidy ball of neatly woven grass with long vertical entrance tunnel extending below.
Length: 16 cm

Cape weaver
Ploceus capensis, Lihlokohloko
Restricted to montane grassland. Usually seen in lightly wooded situations near water, but also in exotic plantations and gardens. Male identified by **olive-greenish upper parts, yellow head and under parts, deep chestnut throat, and pale eye**. Female and non-breeding male drab greenish-brown. Breeds in colonies of up to a dozen pairs. Nest is large conspicuous kidney-shaped structure hanging from lower branches of tree.
Length: 18 cm

Southern masked-weaver
Ploceus velatus, Lihlokohloko
Sparsely distributed in bushveld savanna habitats; highest densities in *Acacia* savanna. Male has **greenish-yellow upper parts, yellow under parts, black mask** extending onto forehead, **pinkish legs and red eye**. Lesser masked-weaver *P. intermedius* has white eye and black legs. Next species has yellow forehead. Female and non-breeding male drab brown. Breeding males build large kidney-shaped nests; only one male per tree.
Length: 16 cm

Village weaver
Ploceus cucullatus, Lihlokohloko
Widespread but absent in the extreme west. Occurs in a variety of wooded habitats. Male identified by **yellow upper parts speckled black, uniform yellow under parts, black mask, and red eye**. Differs from previous species by yellow, not black, forehead. Female and non-breeding male drab brown. Nests in large colonies of dozens of individuals. Male builds typical kidney-shaped nest to attract female to mate with him.
Length: 17 cm

Red-headed weaver
Anaplectes melanotis
Occurs sparsely in the eastern parts of the bush-veld region. Associated with mature woodland, avoiding scrubby, bush-encroached thornveld. Male easily identified by **bright red head, mantle and breast, white belly, olive-yellow wings, and reddish beak**. Female is mostly yellow with white belly and orange beak. Encountered singly or in pairs. Male builds typical messy nest of woven grass with long untidy entrance tunnel.
Length: 15 cm

Red-billed quelea
Quelea quelea, Inyonyane
Occurs sparsely but in very large numbers in the bushveld regions. Usually seen in open savanna, cultivated lands or fallow fields. Roosts in reedbeds. Identified by **drab brown plumage and conspicuous red beak**. Breeding male has variable black facial mask. Forms small to enormous flocks. Has bred on several occasions at Hlane National Park. Nest thin-walled grass ball built by male. Dozens may be situated in single thorn tree.
Length: 12 cm

Southern red bishop
Euplectes orix, Mabhengu
Widespread in suitable wetland habitat. Occurs in reed-beds or rank vegetation in marshes, seasonal pans, flooded wetlands or back waters of dam. Male identified by **bright red upper parts and breast, black face and belly**. Female and non-breeding male drab brown. Breeding male performs aerial display above nest to attract female. Oval nest is thin-walled with side entrance and "porch" woven to stem of reed or bulrush.
Length: 12 cm

Yellow bishop
Euplectes capensis
Restricted to the montane grassland region where it is associated with moist rank vegetation along streams and marshes. Male identified by **black plumage with yellow shoulder patch and yellow rump**. Female and non-breeding male drab brown. An uncommon resident that is most easily seen in small flocks at Malolotja Nature Reserve. Nest is oval with side entrance, and usually placed in low shrub.
Length: 14 cm

GEOFF McILLERON, FIREFLY IMAGES

Fan-tailed widowbird
Euplectes axillaris
Widespread but rare or absent in *Acacia* savanna in the eastern bushveld region. Associated with a variety of habitats but usually in rank vegetation near water, including irrigated fields. Male is easily identified by **all-black plumage with red shoulder patch**. Female and non-breeding male drab brown with pale red shoulder patch. Seen in small flocks. Nest is thin-walled ball of grass placed near the ground in dense vegetation.
Length: 18 cm

GINA JC WILGENBUS

White-winged widowbird
Euplectes albonotatus
Occurs throughout the bushveld regions; highest densities in *Acacia* savanna. Male has **black plumage with yellow and white shoulder patch**. Female and non-breeding male drab brown. Seen in small flocks foraging for seeds on the ground. Male defends a small territory around nest site, displaying continuously to attract females. Nest is thin-walled oval grass ball, woven to vertical stem of tall grass stem in rank vegetation.
Length: 15 cm

GEOFF McILLERON, FIREFLY IMAGES

Red-collared widowbird
Euplectes ardens
Widespread but rare or absent in *Acacia* savanna in the eastern bushveld. Usually in rank vegetation near water, including irrigated fields. Male has **all-black plumage, indistinct red collar and long tail**. Differs from next species by **lack of shoulder patch**. Female and non-breeding male drab brown with pale red shoulder patch. In small flocks. Nest is thin-walled ball of grass placed in herbaceous plant or shrub often near water.
Length: 26 cm

NEIL GRAY

Long-tailed widowbird
Euplectes progne, Sijolobela ♂, Intsaki ♀
Restricted to the montane grassland region. Associated with good quality short grasslands, often near water. Avoids heavily grazed areas. Easily identified by **black plumage, red and white shoulder patch and very long tail**. Differs from previous species by **larger size, longer tail and absence of red collar**. Successful male may breed with several females. Nest is ball of grass placed at base of grass tuft.
Length: 55 cm

Thick-billed weaver
Amblyospiza albifrons
Widespread in suitable habitat, being reed-beds during the breeding season; venturing into woodland at other times. Identified by **dark brown plumage, white wing patches, with thick heavy beak**. Male has white forehead patch. Female is streaked below. Seen in small flocks which may travel long distances between nesting and foraging sites. Nest is unique oval structure made of fine plant matter woven to two reed stems.
Length: 18 cm

PHIL PERRY

 SB   W

Orange-breasted waxbill
Sporaeginthus subflavus
Occurs sparsely in suitable habitat throughout the country. Associated with rank or flooded grassland, marshes and cultivated fields. Male identified by **light brown upper parts, bright yellow under parts, orange breast and vent, and red eye stripe**. Female is drab brown with yellow vent. Occurs in flocks. Flies off a short distance when disturbed then drops back into grass. Usually nests in old bishop or widow nest.
Length: 10 cm

GEOFF McILLERON, FIREFLY IMAGES

G   W

Swee waxbill
Coccopygia melanotis
Occurs in the montane grasslands and highest parts of the Lebombos. Most abundant in the forest/grassland ecotone, but also fallow fields and gardens. Identified by **olive upper parts, pale under parts and red rump**. Male has a black facial mask. Usually in pairs or small groups, but easily overlooked. Nest is oval ball of grass with side entrance low down in bush.

Length: 10 cm

GEOFF McILLERON, FIREFLY IMAGES

G SB L

Common waxbill
Estrilda astrild
One of the most abundant birds in Swaziland. Widespread and associated with rank vegetation near water, but also in fallow fields, cultivated lands and the ecotone between grassland/woodland. Identified by **plain mouse-brown upper parts, paler under parts** and **red mask and red wash on middle of breast**. Usually encountered in small flocks. Nest is scruffy oval mass of grass with side entrance, placed at base of shrub.
Length: 11 cm

MARK D ANDERSON

G   W   SB B   L

MARK D ANDERSON

JACQUES ERARD

MARK D ANDERSON

PETER GINN

Blue waxbill

Uraeginthus angolensis, Intswintswi/Lintjiyane
Very abundant throughout the bushveld. Occurs in various savanna and woodland habitats; highest densities in *Acacia* savanna. Easily identified by **blue under parts and brown upper parts**. Female is slightly duller than male. In pairs when breeding, otherwise in flocks which may number in the hundreds. Forages on the ground for grass seeds. Nest is an untidy ball of grass with side entrance placed in the canopy of a thorny tree.
Length: 12 cm

Pink-throated twinspot

Hypargos margaritatus
Occurs in the bushveld and Lebombo regions. Associated with riparian forest, bushclumps and dense thicket. Male has **pink throat, breast and rump, black belly with white spots and plain brown upper parts**. Female has grey throat, white belly with white spots restricted to flanks. Despite abundance in riparian habitats, it is secretive and difficult to observe. Forages on the forest floor and group members in constant vocal contact.
Length: 13 cm

Green-winged pytilia

Pytilia melba
Restricted to the eastern bushveld. Associated with a range of savanna habitats; highest densities in scrubby *Acacia* savanna. Identified by **olive-green upper parts, grey crown, red rump and finely barred under parts**. Male has conspicuous red throat and forehead. Usually in pairs or small family groups that typically forage on the ground. Nest is untidy ball of grass with side entrance, placed in thorny shrub.
Length: 13 cm

African firefinch

Lagonosticta rubricata
Widespread and common, but scarce in the eastern bushveld. Keeps to thickets and dense undergrowth. Male has **deep pink-red under parts, olive-green upper parts, black vent and black beak**. Red-billed firefinch *L. senegala* has red beak and cream vent. Jameson's firefinch *L. rhodopareia* has pink-red under parts extending onto crown. In small family groups. Nest is grass ball with side entrance in thorny tangle on ground.
Length: 12 cm

Bronze mannikin

Spermestes cucullatus

Very abundant and widespread throughout the country. Associated with wooded habitats including savanna, forest edge, scrub, gardens and fields. Identified by **brown upper parts, black head and throat, and white under parts**. The similar red-backed mannikin *S. bicolor* has deep rufous upper parts. Occurs in small family groups. Nest is untidy ball of grass with side entrance situated in a bush.

Length: 10 cm

PHIL PERRY

SB **B** **L**

Pin-tailed whydah

Vidua macroura, Jojo

Common and widespread in open patches in most wooded situations. Male has **black upper parts and head, white under parts, wing bar and neck, very long tail and red beak**. Female and non-breeding male drab brown with conspicuous black markings on head, and a reddish beak. Breeding male displays incessantly chasing other birds from territory. Eggs laid in the nest of the common waxbill and bronze mannikin.

Length: 13 cm (without tail)

ALAN MANSON

SB **B** **L**

Long-tailed paradise-whydah

Vidua paradisaea

Occurs sparsely in the eastern parts of the bushveld regions. Commonly sighted in *Acacia* savanna. Breeding male easily identified by **black upper parts and head, broad black tail, orange-chestnut under parts and black beak**. Female and non-breeding male drab brown with bold head markings. Breeding male sings from prominent perch, otherwise easily overlooked. Parasitizes green-winged pytilia.

Length: 15 cm (without tail)

GINA JC WILGENBUS

B

Dusky indigobird

Vidua funerea

Occurs sparsely throughout in wooded habitats including forest edge, savanna and edges of cultivated fields. Male has **all-black plumage, red legs and silvery beak**. The very similar village indigobird *V. chalybeata* has a red beak. Female and non-breeding male, drab brown with bold head markings. Male is easily located during the breeding season when it sings from a prominent perch. Parasitises the African firefinch.

Length: 12 cm

Female

ALAN MANSON

SB **B** **L**

PHIL PERRY

Southern grey-headed sparrow
Passer diffusus
Widespread throughout, but sparse in the north-west. Associated with savanna habitats including savanna, woodland, cultivated fields and gardens. Identified by **grey head, mantle and upper back with rufous wings, and paler under parts**. Differs from exotic male house sparrow *P. domesticus* by lack of black throat patch, and from female by brown rump (grey in house sparrow). In pairs or small groups. Nests in hole in tree.
Length: 15 cm

(SB) (B) (L)

GEORGES OLIOSO

Yellow-throated petronia
Petronia superciliaris
Occurs widely throughout the bushveld regions and sparsely in montane grasslands. Associated with wooded habitats; highest densities in *Acacia* savanna. Identified by **warm-brown upper parts, paler under parts with a distinct broad eye stripe**. The yellow throat patch is not visible unless the bird is in the hand. Usually seen in pairs. Forages both on the ground and in the canopy of trees. Nests in tree cavity.
Length: 16 cm

(SB) (B) (L)

GERHARD GELDENHUYS

African pied wagtail
Motacilla aguimp, Umvemve
Occurs in suitable habitat throughout. Associated with large rivers and the shoreline of dams. Identified by **black upper parts and head, white wing bar, white under parts, and clear black breast band**. The mountain wagtail *M. clara* differs by having a longer tail, and greyish plumage. Pairs defend linear territories along water bodies. Nest is untidy mass of grass, roots and leaves resembling debris and is placed in niche in bank.
Length: 20 cm

(W)

PHIL PERRY

Cape wagtail
Motacilla capensis, Umvemve
Occurs widely in montane grasslands and the western bushveld, scarce in other areas. Seen in various open habitats, but usually in grasslands near marshes and streams, and lawns. Has **dirty grey-brown upper parts, white under parts and narrow breast band**. The mountain wagtail *M. clara* has far longer tail and is restricted to fast-flowing mountain streams. Nest bulky mass of grass, roots and leaves placed in niche in bank.
Length: 20 cm

(G) (W)

Yellow-throated longclaw
Macronyx croceus, Licofi
Widespread and present in open grassy areas with scattered trees. Avoids treeless grasslands and bush-encroached savanna. Has mottled brown upper parts, yellow under parts with clear black breast band. Differs from the next species by yellow throat. Usually seen singly or in pairs. Forages by walking on the ground in search of insects, and flies into a tree when disturbed. Nest is bulky mass of grass hidden in dense grass.
Length: 21 cm

PHIL PERRY

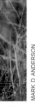

Cape longclaw
Macronyx capensis, Ligwinsi
Restricted to the montane grassland region. Prefers open areas with short grass. Easily identified by **mottled brown upper parts, yellow under parts with clear black breast band**. Differs from the previous species by orange throat. Forages by walking through the grass in search of insects. When disturbed flies off a short distance before dropping back into the grass. Nest is bulky mass of grass well concealed in dense vegetation.
Length: 20 cm

MARK D ANDERSON

African pipit
Anthus cinnamomeus
Occurs widely in suitable habitat throughout the country. Associated with flat, short grasslands and fallow fields. Avoids tall grass or hilly terrain. Pipits are generally difficult to identify. Distinguished by **drab brown body with distinct streaks on the breast**. Differs from long-billed pipit *A. similis* by **white** (not cream) **outer tail feathers**. Call is also distinctive "treeoo, treeoo" uttered in flight. Nest hidden at base of grass tuft.
Length: 17 cm

MARK D ANDERSON

Cape canary
Serinus canicollis
Restricted to the montane grassland region. Associated with scrubby grasslands and exotic plantations. Identified by **yellow under and upper parts**. Distinguished from other canaries by **grey head and nape**. Seen in pairs or small flocks foraging on the ground for grass seeds, flying to tree top when disturbed. Nest is thick-walled woven with herb stems often situated high up in fork of tall tree.
Length: 13 cm

MARK D ANDERSON

SB · B · F · L

Yellow-fronted canary
Crithagra mozambicus, Mbalane
One of the most abundant and widespread species. Occurs in all habitats except treeless grassland and forest interior. Has **yellow under parts, olive-grey upper parts, black malar stripe and yellow eye stripe**. The forest canary *C. scotops* is greenish below with black chin. In pairs when breeding, otherwise in flocks of up to several hundred. Nest is neat, thick-walled cup of grass and roots, built in vertical fork in canopy of tree.
Length: 12 cm

G · SB · L

Streaky-headed seedeater
Crithagra gularis
Occurs widely throughout the country, but absent in the eastern parts of the bushveld regions. Associated with wooded hillsides and exotic plantations. Identified by **drab brown plumage with conspicuous white eye stripe**. Usually solitary or in pairs. Easily overlooked due to drab plumage and quiet nature. Nest is neat cup lined on the outside with bark chips, concealed in fork of tree.

Length: 15 cm

G · SB · L

Cinnamon-breasted bunting
Emberiza tahapisi
Occurs sparsely in rocky outcrops on wooded slopes. Has **rich cinnamon under parts, mottled upper parts, and bold head markings**. Male has black head with white stripes, female has dark brown head with dirty stripes. The Cape bunting *E. capensis* has grey plumage, rufous wings with black facial markings. Seen in pairs foraging on the ground for seeds and insects. Nest is a shallow cup at base of grass tuft or between rocks.
Length: 15 cm

SB · B · L

Golden-breasted bunting
Emberiza flaviventris
Occurs in suitable habitat throughout the country. Associated with various wooded habitats including savanna, woodland, exotic plantations and forest edge. Identified by **rich golden breast, yellow belly, rufous upper parts and boldly marked face**. Usually in pairs foraging on the ground, but sings from a tree. Nest is a thin-walled cup of fine stems situated in a low branch of a shrub or bush.
Length: 15 cm

Freshwater Fishes

Swaziland is a well-watered country with a dense network of tributaries draining into the Komati, Umbuluzi and Usuthu river systems. This results in a wide variety of aquatic habitats and a diverse fish fauna. Due to varied altitude and climate both temperate and subtropical elements occur, the former are found in the western highveld and the latter in the eastern lower lying parts of the country. Fifty-four species have been recorded, representing approximately one fifth of southern Africa's freshwater species. In addition, several alien species have been introduced since the early 1900s. Although some are now presumed extinct, largemouth bass (*Micropterus salmoides*) and rainbow trout (*Oncorhynchus mykiss*) are well established as angling species. Man-made dams support trout (highveld) and bass in the remainder of the country.

Of the fifty-four indigenous species recorded, eighteen of the more common and widespread species are featured here, including snoutfishes, eels, barbs, yellowfishes, labeos, catfishes, rock catlets, cichlids and gobies. Swaziland provides suitable habitat for more than a dozen southern African endemic species, as well as four species that are regionally and globally threatened. This is best illustrated by the occurrence of all six southern African endemic rock catlets (genus *Chiloglanis*). Several indigenous species including tigerfish, yellowfish, barbel and bream provide angling opportunities and about twelve large dams are used by licenced anglers.

Swaziland's fish are threatened by water pollution, both industrial (limited to the Lusushwana River near Matsapha industrial site and the Lusutfu River near Bhunya pulp mill) and agricultural (from fertilisers, insecticides, soil erosion and siltation, due mainly to poor catchment management). In many rivers fish habitats have been altered by dam construction. Water abstraction for irrigation has greatly reduced water flow, affecting fish habitats. The introduction of alien fish species also poses a threat to indigenous fish. Further reading is recommended on page 170.

Southern bulldog
Marcusenius pongoloensis, Nghebe
Occurs in the major rivers and dams in the subtropical bushveld regions. Shows a distinct preference for marginal vegetation and rooted riverbanks. Key features include **the prominent mental lobe jutting forward beyond the snout, deep body with very constricted caudal peduncle and dorsal and anal fins set far back**. An important source of protein for local communities.
Length: 300 mm

ROGER BILLS, SAIAB

W **SB** **B** **L**

Longfin eel
Anguilla mossambica, Mokhane
The most common eel found in river systems, deep pools and headwater streams. Key features include a **uniform pale yellow, brown or grey body with a dirty white belly and the origin of the dorsal fin well in front of the anal fin**. Colour varies with young eels lighter. Three other eels, *A. bengalensis, A. bicolor* and *A. marmorata* occur. Migratory and affected by dam construction. Return to the sea to spawn.
Length: 1.2 m

ROGER BILLS, SAIAB

W

Southern barred minnow

Opsaridium peringueyi
Common and widespread in the Komati, Mbuluzi and Usuthu systems. It prefers pools and riffles below rapids where there is fast flowing, well-aerated water. Also found in runs with a clean sandy substrate. Key features include **the silvery body with several vertical dark bars and the black back edge to the dorsal fin.** Breeding individuals are flushed with pink on the head, body and fins.
Length: 90 mm

Chubbyhead barb

Barbus anoplus
Common and widespread in the upper catchments of the Mbuluzi and Usuthu river systems. One of fifteen small barbs recorded from Swaziland. Restricted to the temperate highveld. Its preferred habitat comprises meandering highveld streams with earth banks and slow flowing pools. Key features include **a blunt head, small mouth, a single pair of barbels and a diffuse stripe on the side of the body.**
Length: 100 mm

Threespot barb

Barbus trimaculatus
Most common barb in Swaziland, widespread in all the major river systems at all altitudes. It occurs in a wide range of habitats including dams, rivers and headwater streams. Key features include **the prominent three black spots on the side of the body and the strong, unserrated dorsal fin spine.** Some individuals may lack one or two of the spots on the side of the body or the spots may be indistinct. It attains a larger size in dams.
Length: 150 mm

Lowveld largescale yellowfish

Labeobarbus marequensis
Common and widespread in all river systems at all altitudes. Generally preferring fast flowing water, the species is also found in large pools and dams. A distinctive yellowfish with a pale yellow to light brown body and pale white belly. Key features include **its large size and large body scales, the latter giving it a low lateral scale count.** Juveniles have a pattern of broken bars on the sides and a dark spot at the base of the tail.
Length: 470 mm

Bushveld smallscale yellowfish

Labeobarbus polylepis

An uncommon species found in the upper catchments of the Komati and Usuthu river systems at altitudes above 600 m. Generally preferring fast flowing water, the species is also found in large pools and dams. The largescale yellowfish (*Labeobarbus marequensis*) occurs in the same waters. Key features distinguishing the species from *L. marequensis* include the **smaller body scales and a higher lateral scale count**.

Length: 460 mm

Leaden labeo

Labeo molybdinus

Common and widespread in all river systems below 1000 m. Occurs in a range of habitats including cascades, bedrock rapids and pools with large rocks. Four other labeos, *L. congoro, L. cylindricus, L. rosae* and *L. ruddi* occur. Of these *L. cylindricus* is the most common and occurs in the same habitat as *L. molybdinus* but can be distinguished by a red eye. *L. rosae* also has a red eye but has a characteristic red nose.

Length: 380 mm

Silver robber

Micralestes acutidens, Sardine

Common in the major river systems in the subtropical bushveld regions. It occurs in clear fast flowing water in medium and large sized rivers, as well as in standing water in dams. Key features include **the small tag-like adipose fin between the dorsal fin and tail, the black-tipped dorsal fin, teeth, silver body and orange coloured tail fin**. Forms large shoals when moving upstream during migrations.

Length: 80 mm

Tigerfish

Hydrocynus vittatus

Uncommon. Recorded from Sivunga and van Eck dams near Big Bend. Occasionally caught in the Lusutfu River. Breeding in the large lowveld rivers probably halted by barrages preventing upstream migration. Key features include **tag-like adipose fin between the dorsal fin and tail, a red tinge to the fins, large sharp teeth and a silver body with dark horizontal stripes**. A popular sport angling species.

Length: 500 mm

W G SB

Stargazer mountain catfish
Amphilius uranoscopus
Common and widespread in all river systems at a range of altitudes apart from the subtropical regions. Occurs in rivers in mountainous and hilly terrain preferring rocky stream habitats where bedrock and loose rocks are present. A rare species, *A. natalensis*, occurs in headwater streams in the highveld. Key features include **a short spineless dorsal fin, flattened head and wide terminal mouth with three pairs of barbels**.
Length: 500 mm

W B

Silver catfish
Schilbe intermedius
Restricted to, but common at, some sites in the lower lying subtropical bushveld region. It prefers open water habitats in large rivers and dams. Key features include **a small adipose fin located between the dorsal and caudal fins, dorsal and pectoral fins with sharp spines, flattened head and a narrow terminal mouth with four pairs of barbels**. An important source of protein for local communities.
Length: 300 mm

W

Sharptooth catfish
Clarias gariepinus, Bhabuli
Common and widespread in all the major river systems below 1000 m. Occurs in still water with marginal vegetation in a variety of river and dam habitats and in vegetated side pools of mountain streams. Another catfish, *C. ngamensis*, occurs in dams in the lowveld. Key features include **a large bony head, wide mouth with four pairs of long barbels and large size**. Popular for angling and a protein source for local communities.
Length: 1.4 m

W

Swaziland rock catlet
Chiloglanis emarginatus
Common and widespread in all the major river systems at a range of altitudes in rocky stream habitats with cascades and rapids. Five other species of *Chiloglanis* occur, some having specific habitat requirements, eg *C. anoterus* is restricted to the temperate highveld region. Key features include **a dorsal fin with a sharp spine, a flattened head and a large suctorial mouth enabling attachment to rocks in fast flowing water**.
Length: 70 mm

Southern mouthbrooder

Pseudocrenilabrus philander

Common and widespread in all the major river systems below 1000 m. Occurs in a wide range of habitats such as fast flowing side channels, isolated vegetated pools and stagnant standing water. Key features include **a series of vertical bands on the body, a rounded tail fin and small size**. Breeding males are colourful with a yellow body and pink fins. Females mouthbrood eggs and fry.

Length 130 mm

Redbreast tilapia

Tilapia rendalli

Common in all major river systems in subtropical bushveld regions. Prefers quiet vegetated habitats in the lower reaches of larger rivers, but also found in dams. Another tilapia, *T. sparrmanii*, occurs in similar habitat in the temperate highveld region. ***T. rendalli* has a bright red breast and 5 to 7 broad vertical bars on the body while *T. sparrmanii* has 8 to 9 narrower vertical bars on the body and darkly pigmented pelvic fins.**

Length 400 mm

Mozambique tilapia

Oreochromis mossambicus, Sikhwalakhwala

Common and widespread in all major river systems in all regions. Occurs in a wide range of habitats such as fast flowing side channels, isolated vegetated pools, stagnant standing water and large dams. Key features include **three dark spots on the side of the body in non-breeding individuals. Breeding males are blue-black with red fringes to the fins.** An important aquaculture species and protein source for local communities.

Length: 400 mm

Tank goby

Glossogobius giuris, Mehlwenhloko

Restricted to, and uncommon at, river and dam sites in the subtropical bushveld regions. Occurs in a variety of habitats from clear rocky pools in slow-flowing rivers to large turbid dams with a muddy substrate. Can be locally common. Another goby, *G. callidus,* also occurs in similar habitats and can be distinguished from *G. giuris* by a **double dark spot at the base of the tail, a more slender build and smaller size**.

Length: 120 mm

Amphibians

There is a wide variety of aquatic and terrestrial habitats in Swaziland. The amphibian fauna is composed of temperate and subtropical components, with the former occurring in the western highveld and the latter in the lower lying eastern parts. The amphibian fauna is diverse with 44 species being recorded, representing approximately one third of all the species found in southern Africa. Twenty-six of these are featured here.

Swaziland's frogs are threatened by habitat loss, this has probably led to the extinction of the giant bullfrog in the highveld. Another highveld species, the yellow-striped reed frog, is facing local extinction due to alien plant invasion of its specific habitat. Available frog habitats are reduced by extensive monocultures and the draining of natural pans in the wake of agricultural development. Dams transform and reduce the variety of frog habitats. Industrial pollution in rivers poses another threat.

Most frogs require water for breeding and return each year to their breeding sites. Not all frogs breed in water and Swaziland has four species that are direct developers, these lay their eggs in an underground nest and the tadpoles complete their development inside the egg before emerging as perfect replicas of the adults. Frogs can produce a cacophony of different sounds and each species has a unique mating call. You can easily determine the number of species at a breeding site by identifying their calls. Tracking down frogs by homing in on their calls is best done at night during or after rain. The majority of species are summer breeding and begin calling from August through to February, while the winter breeding species start to call as the first chills of autumn occur, usually in late March.

Swaziland has some remarkable frogs: tree frogs that build foam nests in trees, burrowing frogs that carry tadpoles on their bodies, colourful reed frogs, noisy toads, grass frogs that are extreme leapers, small dainty frogs and the elusive and mysterious ghost frog. Further reading is recommended on page 170.

W

Common platanna
Xenopus laevis, Siphata
Common. Widespread throughout all regions. Occurs in most types of water body. Totally aquatic, it lives, feeds and breeds in water. Call is a soft buzzing sound. Key features include **the flattened body, extensive webbing of the hind-feet and claws on the toes**. The subtropical platanna (*X. muelleri*) occurs in the subtropical regions and is absent from the temperate highveld. Has a long subocular tentacle below the eye.
Length: 86 mm

W F G

Natal ghost frog
Heleophryne natalensis
A rare species restricted to the temperate highveld. Occurs in clear, perennial, swift-flowing mountain streams flowing through indigenous forest. **Adults are squat with discs on their fingers and toes, and tadpoles have large sucker mouths**. These are adaptive features for gripping onto rocks. Tadpoles take two years to develop into frogs. The high-pitched "pinging" call can be heard from March to May near waterfalls.
Length: 60 mm

Guttural toad
Bufo gutturalis
Common and widespread throughout all regions.
Occurs in a wide range of habitats and frequently
breeds in man-made dams and garden ponds. Call
is a long guttural snore. Can be confused with the
olive toad (*Bufo garmani*). **Both have pink colouring on the thighs.** *B. gutturalis* **has a characteristic light coloured cross between the eyes
and snout.** *B. garmani* is a subtropical species
and is absent from the highveld.
Length: 96 mm

Raucous toad
Bufo rangeri
An uncommon species restricted to the temperate highveld region. Occurs in montane grassland and savanna habitats above 900 m. Breeds in
still pools in rivers and occasionally in man-made
dams. Call is a repetitive duck-like quack. Key
features include **no pink markings on the thighs
and a uniformly coloured snout.** Attains a larger size than the guttural toad that is found in the
same habitat.
Length: 106 mm

Flatbacked toad
Bufo maculatus
Common and widespread in subtropical bushveld,
absent from temperate highveld. Occurs in medium to large rivers favouring fast flowing water
and rapids. Not known to breed in man-made habitats. Call is a loud repetitive quack produced from
cover. Can be confused with common guttural
toad *(Bufo gutturalis)*. Key features include **poorly developed parotid glands behind the eye,
hence the common name, and its smaller size.**
Length: 65 mm

Red toad
Schismaderma carens
Common and widespread but less common in the
highveld. Occurs in a wide range of habitats, preferring savanna and bushveld. Frequently breeds
in man-made dams and ponds. Call is a drawn out
booming like a revving motorcycle engine. Key
features include **no glands behind the eyes and
a uniform red, pale pink or grey colour with
small paired darker markings on the back.** The
black tadpoles form a swarming ball.
Length: 84 mm

111

Bushveld rain frog

Breviceps adspersus, Sinana

Common and widespread in the subtropical regions, absent from the temperate highveld. Prefers sandy regions in bushveld habitats where they can burrow into the ground. Has **a round body, short stubby legs and no neck.** Moves around during or after rain. *B. verrucosus* occurs in highveld forest, *B. mossambicus* in grassland and *B. sopranus* in Lebombo scrub savanna. Eggs are laid underground and hatch directly into frogs.
Length: 47 mm

SB B L

Banded rubber frog

Phrynomantis bifasciatus

Common and widespread subtropical species in the eastern parts, absent from the temperate highveld. Breeds in temporary pans and flooded quarries and borrow pits. Produces a high-pitched trilling call audible from a kilometre or more. Calls from the base of grass tussocks at the water's edge. Key features include **elongated body, short head, short limbs and contrasting red or pale pink and black colouring.**
Length: 56 mm

W SB B L

Mottled burrowing frog

Hemisus marmoratus

Common in subtropical regions in bushveld and savanna habitats. Absent from the highveld. Breeds in flooded pans, quarries and borrow pits. Call is a high-pitched continuous buzz similar to a cricket. Has **a sharply pointed snout, round body, and short limbs.** Burrows headfirst into the ground. Eggs are laid in a hole at the edge of the pan. If the nest is not flooded the tadpoles are carried to the water on the female's body.
Length: 39 mm

W SB B L

Common river frog

Afrana angolensis, Indlonja

Common and widespread throughout all regions and altitudes in a wide range of habitats. Often breeds in man-made dams and garden ponds. Call is a long rattling sound ending in a short croak. Breeds mainly in winter but also in summer when cold fronts occur. Has **a sharply pointed snout**, dark patches on the body and (usually) **a bright yellow vertebral stripe**. Tadpoles are large (80 mm) and take up to three years to develop.
Length: 80 mm

W

Striped stream frog
Strongylopus fasciatus
Uncommon and restricted to the temperate high-veld. Occurs in reed-beds along streams and around natural vleis in montane grassland and around man-made dams. Winter breeding, but also calls in summer during cold fronts. Call is a high-pitched single 'pip' or a ripple of three or more 'pips'. Has **a sharply pointed snout, long hindlimbs and unwebbed toes**. Another species *S. grayii* occurs in streams in highveld forest.
Length: 40 mm

Sharp-nosed grass frog
Ptychadena oxyrhynchus
Common and widespread in grassland and bush-veld habitats including streams, grassy pans, flooded quarries and borrow pits and dams. Call consists of a series of high-pitched trills peaking after midnight. Two other *Ptychadena* species occur in the same habitat, while another species is restricted to grassy seepage areas in the temperate highveld. They have **a sharply pointed snout and large hindlimbs**. Exceptional leapers.
Length: 60 mm

Plain grass frog
Ptychadena anchietae
Common and widespread throughout the sub-tropical regions in a wide range of bushveld habitats including rivers and seasonal pans, and also in flooded quarries, borrow pits and dams. Call consists of a series of high-pitched trills peaking after midnight. Occurs in the same bushveld habitats as *P. oxyrhynchus*. Has **a uniform brown to red body with a pale triangular patch on the snout**. An exceptional leaper.
Length: 53 mm

African bullfrog
Pyxicephalus edulis
Uncommon. Found in the subtropical regions, absent from the temperate highveld. Occurs in temporary pans, flooded quarries and borrow pits in bushveld habitats and in roadside drainage ditches. Call is a short low-pitched bellow. Has **prominent skin ridges on the back, a solid body shape and short muscular limbs**. The giant bull-frog (*P. adspersus*), a highveld species, became extinct in the 1980s due to habitat loss.
Length: 103 mm

Natal sand frog
Tomopterna natalensis
Common and widespread. Occurs in a wide range of habitats preferring sandy areas. Breeds in shallow sandy streams, seepages and shallow rock pools. Produces a penetrating, monotonous, high-pitched call audible from a kilometre or more. The call often starts with a few 'chirrups'. Two other species occur in the subtropical regions. Both have a more stubby build than *T. natalensis* and attain a larger size (51 mm).
Length: 40 mm

Ornate burrowing frog
Hildebrandtia ornata
Restricted to the subtropical bushveld regions, absent from the temperate highveld. Occurs in temporary pans and flooded grassy depressions. Call is a loud coarse honking sound produced every two-seconds. Swaziland's most beautiful frog. Key features include **striking striped green, orange and grey pattern and pale Y-shaped markings on the throat**. A burrowing species that emerges after heavy rain.
Length: 70 mm

Common caco
Cacosternum boettgeri
Common and widespread but less common in the highveld. Occurs in a wide range of habitats, preferring grassy inundated areas and temporary pans. Also found in farm dams. The rasping call is like the sound made when winding up a clock. **The colour patterns of these dainty little frogs range from green to brown with or without thin vertebral stripes**. Two other species occur. *C. nanum* (widespread) and *C. parvum* (highveld).
Length: 26 mm

Snoring puddle frog
Phrynobatrachus natalensis
Common and widespread throughout all regions in a wide range of habitats. Call is a distinctive drawn out snore. Key features include **a short, blunt snout and a nondescript uniform brown, grey or black body with or without a thin or broad yellow stripe or band down the back**. Another much smaller (19 mm) species, *P. mabiensis,* occurs in similar habitats. Its call is a long high-pitched "buzz" ending in "tick - tick".
Length: 33 mm

Foam nest tree frog

Chiromantis xerampelina

Restricted to the subtropical regions. It occurs in savanna and bushveld habitats and breeds in temporary pans, flooded quarries and borrow pits and along rivers. A foam nest is made from beating the albumin produced during egg-laying with the hindlimbs. The outer layer hardens and the tadpoles hatch in the nest and drop out of the bottom of the nest into the water below. **Adults can be seen sitting near their nests.**

Length: 84 mm

Brown-backed tree frog

Leptopelis mossambicus

A fairly common and widespread subtropical species that is absent from the temperate highveld. Occurs along wooded drainage lines, around temporary pans and in man-made habitats such as dams, flooded quarries and borrow pits. Call is a short gruff quack usually produced while the frog is in a tree or shrub 1 to 2 metres above the ground. It has **a dark brown patch on the back and terminal discs on fingers and toes**.

Length: 58 mm

Bubbling kassina

Kassina senegalensis

Common and widespread throughout all regions and habitats. Call is a distinctive "oink" with long intervals. Starts calling in late afternoon some distance away from the water moving closer as nightfall approaches. Has **an elongated body and short limbs.** Prefers to walk or run than to hop. The subtropical species *K. maculata* has bright red colouring in the groin area and a loud watery "quack" call produced every second.

Length: 45 mm

Long-toed running frog

Semnodactylus wealii

An uncommon species restricted to the highveld region. Occurs primarily in seepage areas in montane grassland but also in grassy man-made dams and flooded borrow pits. Call is a drawn out "creak-pop" with long intervals between calls. It calls from an elevated position in a shrub or grass tussock some distance away from the water. Key features include **a black and caramel striped pattern, short limbs and long toes**.

Length: 43 mm

RICHARD BOYCOTT

(W) (SB) (B) (L)

Golden leaf-folding frog
Afrixalus aureus
Common and widespread in subtropical areas, absent from the highveld. Prefers grassy areas by rivers and temporary pans. Also found in grassy man-made habitats such as quarries, drainage ditches and dams. Call is a high-pitched "tsik". Eggs are laid on a leaf surface and the leaf is folded and glued by the hindfeet of the mating pair to form a tube, thereby hiding the eggs. Has **an elongated head and body and short hindlimbs.**
Length: 25 mm

RICHARD BOYCOTT

(W) (G)

Yellow-striped reed frog
Hyperolius semidiscus
Uncommon species restricted to the temperate highveld. Favours deep pools at the bottom of waterfalls along medium to large highveld rivers flowing through montane grassland. Call is a series of harsh creaks descending in frequency. Has **a bright yellow stripe along sides of green body and pink discs on tips of fingers and toes**. The green reed frog, *H. tuberilinguis*, occurs in the subtropical regions and lacks the yellow stripe.
Length: 37 mm

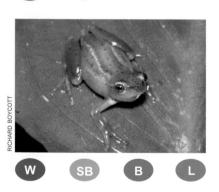

RICHARD BOYCOTT

(W) (SB) (B) (L)

Water lily frog
Hyperolius pusillus
Common and widespread in the subtropical bushveld regions. Occurs in a wide variety of habitats including temporary pans and flooded depressions as well as man-made habitats such as quarries, borrow pits and dams. Favours habitats with water lilies. Call is a high-pitched electric buzz. Key features include **uniform green colour, almost translucent body and small size**. Occurs with *H. marmoratus* and *H. tuberilinguis* at some sites.
Length: 23 mm

RICHARD BOYCOTT

(W)

Painted reed frog
Hyperolius marmoratus
Common and widespread throughout, less common in the temperate highveld. Occurs in a wide variety of habitats over a range of altitudes. Call comprises a series of several high pitched whistles produced at one second intervals. Deafening choruses are formed by large populations of frogs. Has **bright yellow and black longitudinal stripes and dull red fore and hindfeet**. Occurs with *H. semidiscus* at some highveld sites.
Length: 34 mm

Reptiles

Swaziland's varied topography and climate provide a wide variety of habitats for reptiles with both temperate and subtropical elements occurring, the former in the western highveld and the latter in the subtropical bushveld. The reptile fauna is composed of 111 species (of which 50 are featured here), including one crocodile, five chelonians (tortoises and terrapins), 44 lizards and 61 snakes. Swaziland has about a quarter of the total southern African fauna, and 35 species found in the country are endemic to the sub-continent. Swaziland has one endemic and two near-endemic reptiles. The giant Swazi flat gecko is found nowhere else, and the Barberton girdled lizard and Swazi rock snake occur marginally in adjacent South Africa.

Swaziland's reptiles are under threat from several factors leading to habitat transformation and loss. Two of Swaziland's reptiles, the python and crocodile, are threatened primarily through persecution and secondly through loss of habitat. Several others are on the brink of being categorized as threatened. The helmeted terrapin has become locally extinct in the highveld because of the destruction of seasonal pans through cultivation and fires. Annually many reptiles are killed on the roads and through burning of the veld.

Reptiles are found in a wide range of habitats from pristine ecosystems to suburban and urban areas. Fortunately, only seven out of 61 of the snakes found in Swaziland are highly venomous and can be considered dangerous to humans. The Big Seven (☠) are the puff adder, Mozambique spitting cobra, snouted cobra, rinkhals, black mamba, boomslang and vine snake. Not all seven occur in the same habitat, although most of them are found in the subtropical bushveld.

Reptiles are more active in the summer months and start moving around during the first spring rains and when temperatures increase. They reproduce by laying eggs or by giving birth to live young. Some reptiles look after their eggs until they hatch (crocodiles and pythons), while others simply lay their eggs or give birth and move on. Further reading is recommended on page 170.

SNAKES

Puff adder (☠)
Bitis arietans, Libululu

Occurs throughout all regions in a wide range of habitats. Potentially the most dangerous snake because it is heavy bodied and cannot move out of the way quickly. Relies on camouflage to avoid detection but if trodden on, will not hesitate to bite. Feeds on small mammals and birds. Key features include **the wide, flat head very distinct from the neck and, down the back, a series of dark chevrons pointing to the tail**.
Length: 1.1 m

G SB B L

Mozambique spitting cobra (☠)
Naja mossambica, Imfeti

Common and widespread throughout but less common in the temperate highveld. This snake and the puff adder are responsible for most serious snakebites. Feeds primarily on amphibians (especially toads) but also favours small mammals and birds. Key features include **the spreading of a hood and a black and salmon pink band across the throat**. Can spit venom up to three metres at any threatening movement.
Length: 1.3 m

G SB B L W

117

Black mamba (☠)

Dendroaspis polylepis, Imamba

Occurs in bushveld and savanna habitats in the warmer lower-lying regions of the country. Also occurs in river valleys that penetrate the highveld such as the Komati and Great Usutu. The mamba has a fearsome reputation that it hardly deserves. It is potentially highly dangerous but prefers to move off if possible. Key features include **its large size and black interior of the mouth.**

Length: 4.0 m

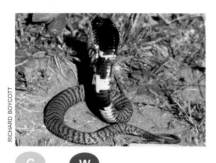

Rinkhals (☠)

Hemachatus haemachatus, Phemphetfwane

Uncommon and restricted to the temperate highveld. Occurs in montane grassland habitats usually close to water. Can spit its venom but needs first to stand up and spread a hood. As a last resort this snake shams death in the hope that it might be left alone and then escape. Feeds on amphibians and small mammals. A key feature is **the long broad hood presenting a black and white banded throat towards its attacker.**

Length: 1.3 m

Snouted cobra (☠)

Naja annulifera, Phemphetfwane

Uncommon subtropical species absent from the temperate highveld. Patchy distribution in bushveld habitats mostly in eastern Swaziland. Has **a solid build, large size and uniform dull yellow or dark brown body.** Older specimens are darker in colour. Primarily nocturnal it will start moving around in the late afternoon but does emerge from hiding to bask in the sun during the day. Feeds on small mammals, birds and other snakes.

Length: 2.5 m

Boomslang (☠)

Dispholidus typus, Indlondlo

Widespread but more common in the subtropical regions. Occurs in a wide range of habitats at all altitudes where there are trees. Restricted to riverine thickets and bushy rock outcrops in montane grassland in the temperate highveld but can be found anywhere in bushveld regions. Key features include **the very large eye and the small head that is distinct from the neck.** Males are usually green, females brown, grey or black.

Length: 2.0 m

Vine snake (☠)

Thelotornis capensis, Lununkhu
Uncommon and widespread, occurs in a wide range of habitats at all altitudes where there are trees. Restricted to wooded outcrops in montane grassland. Found anywhere in bushveld regions. A very well camouflaged snake that **looks like a dead branch** and one of a few snakes that can see immobile prey. Feeds on birds, lizards and amphibians. Key features include **the elongated flat head, slender body and exceptionally long tail**.
Length: 1.5 metres

Southern African python

Python natalensis, Inhlatfu
Uncommon throughout the warmer subtropical regions and absent from the highveld. Occurs in a wide variety of habitats favouring rocky areas and thick bush near water. Also found in modified habitats such as sugar cane plantations. A **large conspicuous snake** frequently persecuted by humans. Feeds on mammals and birds using its constricting powers to overcome its prey. Plays an important role in controlling vermin.
Length: 5.0 m

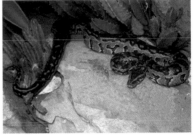

Bibron's blind snake

Typhlops bibronii
Widespread throughout the country, most common in the temperate highveld region. Occurs in a variety of habitats preferring moist soils. A locally common burrowing snake often found sheltering under rocks or in termite nests. It is nocturnal and feeds on termites and their eggs. Key features include **a rounded head and tail, a spade like snout for burrowing and no visible eyes**.

Length: 500 mm

Common brown water snake

Lycodonomorphus rufulus
Widespread throughout the country and more common in the temperate highveld region. Occurs in a variety of moist habitats never very far from water. Feeds on frogs, which are overpowered by constriction. Primarily a nocturnal snake but does hunt for tadpoles in streams and pools during the day. Key features include **the uniform dark brown to black body, with pale undersides sometimes coloured yellow or pink**.
Length: 700 mm

119

G

Olive house snake
Lamprophis inornatus
Common and widespread in the temperate high-veld region. Occurs in a variety of natural habitats in montane grassland but also found around houses and outbuildings. Feeds on small mammals and lizards that are constricted before being swallowed. A useful ally in the control of rats and mice in gardens and storerooms. Has **a distinct python-like head and a uniform olive green or grey body with pale undersides**.
Length: 1.0 m

G   SB   B   L

Brown house snake
Lamprophis capensis, Umdlume
Common and widespread but less common in the highveld. Occurs in a variety of natural habitats and found around houses and outbuildings. Feeds on small mammals that are constricted before being swallowed. A useful ally in the control of rats and mice in gardens and storerooms. Has **a distinct python-like head, a uniform red to dark brown body and distinct white stripes passing through the eyes onto the side of the head**.
Length: 800 mm

G

Swazi rock snake
Lamprophis swazicus
A rare snake confined to the temperate highveld region. It occurs in rocky outcrops and ridges in undulating montane grassland and is also found under large flat rocks. An excellent rock-climber, it is active at dusk and after dark when seeking out sleeping diurnal lizards in rock cracks. Also feeds on geckos that are active at night. Key features include **broad flattened head, distinct from the neck and long slender body**.
Length: 900 mm

SB   B   L

Cape file snake
Mehelya capensis, Imamba lukhonkhotse
Fairly common and widespread in the subtropical regions and absent from the temperate highveld. Occurs in a wide range of savanna, woodland and bushveld habitats. Feeds on a variety of other snakes including venomous species over powering these by constriction. Key features include **triangular body shape, broad flattened head with small eyes and prominent white ridge down the centre of the back**.
Length: 1.5 m

Common slug-eater

Duberria lutrix

Common and widespread in the temperate high-veld, restricted to this region. Occurs in a wide range of moist montane grassland habitats. Also occurs in suburban gardens and parks. It feeds on slugs and snails thereby providing a very useful service to gardeners. Has **a small head not very distinct from the neck, the russet to dark brown body with grey sides and the pale yellow belly**. Rolls into a tight spiral in defence.

Length: 400 mm

G

Mole snake

Pseudaspis cana, Imboma

Uncommon and widespread in all regions, more common in the temperate highveld. Occurs in a variety of grassland, savanna and bushveld habitats. Also found in man-altered habitats like farmland and riding stables. A useful snake as it feeds on problem animals such as moles, rats and mice. Key features include **sharply pointed snout, and small head that is not distinct from the neck**.

Length: 1.5 m

G   SB   B   L

Short-snouted grass snake

Psammophis brevirostris

Common and widespread in grassland, savanna and bushveld habitats. Three other grass snakes are found: *P. mossambicus* occurs in the same habitat as *P. brevirostris*; *P. crucifer* is confined to highveld grassland and *P. subtaeniatus* to subtropical Lebombo bushveld. Very alert and quick moving all feed primarily on lizards but will also eat small mammals, birds and snakes. All possess mild venom of little consequence to humans.

Length: 1.2 m

G   SB   B   L

Green water snake

Philothamnus hoplogaster

Common and widespread throughout all regions. Occurs in a range of grassland, savanna and bushveld habitats. Also found in suburban gardens and parks. A nervous and alert diurnal snake that feeds on lizards and frogs. Can be confused with the next species, *P. natalensis*. Key features include **a uniform lime green body, pale undersides and its small size**.

Length: 600 mm

G   SB   B   L

121

Natal green snake
Philothamnus natalensis
Uncommon and widespread throughout all regions. In the temperate highveld it occurs along forested rivers and, in the subtropical regions, in riverine thicket. A nervous and alert diurnal snake that is more arboreal than the green water snake. Key features include **uniform green body with small blue flecks, yellow-green sides and pale underside**. It attains a larger size than *P. hoplogaster.*
Length: 1.3 m

Spotted bush snake
Philothamnus semivariegatus
Common and widespread, it occurs in a wide range of grassland, savanna and bushveld habitats. It is arboreal and spends most of the time in bushes and trees. A nervous and agile snake that feeds primarily on lizards (geckos and chameleons) but also eats frogs. It has **black variegated markings on the front portion of the body, fading towards the uniformly coloured tail, and large eyes set in an elongated head**.
Length: 1.3 m

Herald snake
Crotaphopeltis hotamboeia
Common and widespread in grassland, savanna and bushveld habitats usually near water. Nocturnal, it feeds on frogs and toads. Key features include **black colour to the back and sides of the head, pale upper lip area and uniform olive green or grey body**. When the skin on the back and sides is stretched tiny white flecks are visible. Threatens by flattening the head and striking out. Has mild venom.
Length: 800 mm

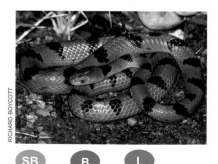

Eastern tiger snake
Telescopus semiannulatus
Uncommon and widespread in the subtropical regions and absent from the temperate highveld. Occurs in a range of savanna and bushveld habitats. A nocturnal snake that feeds on small mammals, including bats, lizards and small birds. Key features include **a broad head that is distinct from the neck, large eyes and numerous black crossbars down the back**. The mild venom is of little consequence to humans.
Length: 1.0 m

Common egg-eater
Dasypeltis scabra

Common and widespread, most common in the highveld. Occurs in a wide range of grassland, savanna and bushveld habitats. Nocturnal, it feeds exclusively on birds eggs. Puts on an impressive threat display by rubbing its body coils together producing a rasping sound not unlike a hiss and striking out with open mouth. Has **rough, keeled body scales, rhombic markings down the back and a black interior of the mouth**.

Length: 1.1 m

Cape centipede-eater
Aparallactus capensis

Uncommon and widespread, but more common in the highveld. Occurs in a wide range of grassland, savanna and bushveld habitats. Often found under rocks in grassland and hibernates in termite nests. Preys exclusively on centipedes by first chewing the centipede along the length of the body before swallowing it head first. Key features include **a slender body, the black head that obscures the small eyes and a black collar**. Has mild venom.

Length: 400 mm

Common night adder
Causus rhombeatus

Common and widespread in the highveld. Prefers damp locations in grassland and savanna habitats. Feeds exclusively on frogs and toads. Bites its prey and waits until the venom takes effect before swallowing it, usually headfirst. Has **a 'V' marking on the head pointing towards the snout and rhombic markings down the back**. Venom is mild to humans. The smaller snouted night adder, *C. defilippii,* occurs in savanna regions.

Length: 800 mm

LIZARDS

Giant Swazi flat gecko
Afroedura major

Uncommon in the highveld and western subtropical bushveld. Endemic to Swaziland. Recently listed as "Near Threatened" due to habitat loss, specifically in the Maguga Dam basin. It occurs in large boulder clumps in mountainous terrain and cliff faces along rivers. **A large nocturnal gecko with a dark "W" shaped mark on the back of the head, flattened body and enlarged paired digital pads.**

Length: 157 mm

123

RICHARD BOYCOTT

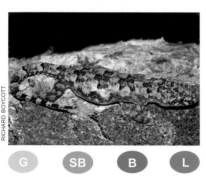

RICHARD BOYCOTT

JOHAN MARAIS

PHIL PERRY

Cape dwarf gecko
Lygodactylus capensis
Common and widespread. Rupicolous and arboreal it occurs in a wide variety of habitats, at all altitudes. An active diurnal gecko. Another species *L. ocellatus* is restricted to granite and ironstone rock outcrops in the temperate highveld. Key features include **conspicuous white and black stripes passing from snout through the eye and along the flanks. Also has elongated digital pads on all four feet.**
Length: 76 mm

G **SB** **B** **L** **F**

Moreau's tropical house gecko
Hemidactylus mabouia
Common and widespread throughout but less common in the temperate highveld. Rupicolous and arboreal it occurs in a wide variety of habitats, at all altitudes. Nocturnal. Also found around buildings and houses where it forages for insects attracted by outside lights. It is expanding its range into urban areas. Has **a flat almost translucent body and digital pads with retractile claws.**
Length: 120 mm

G **SB** **B** **L**

Wahlberg's velvet gecko
Homopholis wahlbergii
Common and widespread throughout but less common in the temperate highveld. Rupicolous and arboreal it occurs in a wide variety of habitats, at all altitudes. Also forages at night around buildings and houses for insects, often with *Hemidactylus mabouia*. A large conspicuous nocturnal gecko. Has **a loose velvety skin (which tears easily), large digital pads and large size**.

Length: 200 mm

G **SB** **B** **L**

Southern tree agama
Acanthocercus atricollis, Intfulo
Common and widespread. Arboreal in subtropical regions and rupicolous in highveld. Basks on tree trunks and large boulders. Males are very conspicuous with their bright blue head. A large active diurnal lizard. May forage on the ground but will take refuge in trees when threatened, remaining on the opposite side of the tree trunk to the danger. Characterised by **spiny body scales, box-shaped head and large size**.
Length: 275 mm

G **SB** **B** **L**

Distant's ground agama

Agama aculeata distanti, Holoholo

Common and widespread in the highveld and subtropical middleveld. Occurs in rocky terrain in montane grassland and sour bushveld. A relic population occurs on the Lebombo plateau. Small and terrestrial, they may climb onto low rocks. Often seen basking on paths and dirt tracks. Feeds on termites, ants and other invertebrates. Has **small spiny scales on the head and back, box-shaped head, stubby build and short tail**.

Length: 186 mm

G SB L

Flap-neck chameleon

Chamaeleo dilepis, Lunwabu

Common and widespread but less common in the highveld. Occurs in wooded grassland but is more common in subtropical bushveld, especially in *Acacia* thornveld. Primarily arboreal, it descends to hibernate under rocks (in the highveld) and to dig a hole to lay its eggs. It feeds on insects, especially grasshoppers and beetles. Has **turreted eyes, clasping feet (with opposable toes), prehensile tail and deep body shape**.

Length: 170 mm

G SB B L

Swazi dwarf chameleon

Bradypodion species, Lunwabu

Restricted to the highveld region, absent from the rest of the country. Occurs in montane grassland and indigenous forest. During the day can be seen on fences and telephone wires, and sometimes crossing roads. At night can be found resting on reeds along the banks of rivers or dams. Feeds on flying insects. Has **turreted eyes, clasping feet (with opposable toes), prehensile tail and shallow elongated body shape**.

Length: 170 mm

G

Rainbow skink

Trachylepis margaritifer

Common and widespread but absent from the highveld above 1 000 m. A rupicolous lizard that favours rocky habitats, especially along rivers. Males are brightly coloured in bronze with tinges of orange and red on the flanks while females and juveniles have a black and yellow longitudinal striped pattern. Very agile diurnal lizards. Has **smooth shiny body scales, short legs, yellow (males) or blue (females) tail, and large size**.

Length: 280 mm

G SB B L

RICHARD BOYCOTT

G   SB   B   L

Variable skink

Trachylepis varia

Common and widespread, probably the most common lizard in the country. Associated with rocks in grassland, savanna, woodland and bushveld at all altitudes. Also found in degraded and transformed habitats and often takes up residence in suburban gardens. Characterised by **a distinct white stripe that extends from the snout along the length of the body, passing below the eye and above the base of the limbs, onto the tail**.

Length: 160 mm

JOHAN MARAIS

G

Montane speckled skink

Trachylepis punctatissima

Common and widespread in the temperate highveld region absent from the subtropical bushveld regions. Occurs in a variety of natural and man-made habitats. The fatter common striped skink (*T. striata*) occurs in the subtropical bushveld regions. Both characterised by a **distinct bronze (*punctatissima*) or yellow (*striata*) stripe** that extends along the body from just in front of the eye, over the eyebrow, to the base of the tail.

Length: 200 mm

RICHARD BOYCOTT

G   SB   B   L

Giant legless skink

Acontias plumbeus

Common and widespread in temperate grassland and savanna habitats but is also found in subtropical bushveld habitats where there are deep soils. Primarily fossorial, it surfaces when the ground becomes waterlogged. A large distinctive purple-black legless lizard it is often misidentified as a snake. Feeds on large invertebrates and newborn mice. Has **a large girth, prominent hard pointed snout and blunt-tipped cylindrical tail**.

Length: 500 mm

PHIL PERRY

G   SB   B   L

Rock monitor

Varanus albigularis, Imbulu

Common and widespread where there are rock outcrops and cliff faces or large trees. A large conspicuous lizard often seen crossing roads. It feeds on a wide range of prey including invertebrates, small rodents, ground dwelling birds and other reptiles such as baby tortoises. Has **a swollen snout with the nostril slits being closer to the eyes than the end of the snout, a large powerful tail and sharp claws on the feet**.

Length: 1.7 m

Nile monitor
Varanus niloticus, Chamu
Common and widespread in a wide range of
aquatic habitats. Basks on rock ledges and will
climb trees. A large conspicuous lizard that swims
well. It feeds on carrion and a variety of prey including invertebrates, small rodents, fish, amphibians and other reptiles such as baby terrapins. Has
**a narrow, elongated head with the nostril slits
closer to the snout than the eyes, a laterally
flattened tail and sharp claws on the feet**.
Length: 2.2 m

Giant plated lizard
Gerrhosaurus validus
Uncommon and widespread in subtropical bushveld. Occurs on rocky ridges, rock outcrops and
in boulder strewn bushveld country. Very seldom
ventures far from its retreat under a rock or in a
rock crevice. Feeds primarily on invertebrates but
also takes plant material such as flowers and fruit.
Has **plate-like body scales, and a thin pale white
stripe extending from behind the head along
the sides of the back to the base of the tail**.
Length: 600 mm

Cape grass lizard
Chamaesaura anguina
Common and widespread in the temperate highveld. Occurs in montane grassland areas that are
not subject to annual fires. Highly specialised lizards with an elongated snake-like body that ena-
bles them to move rapidly through grass. Three
species are in Swaziland, two found in montane
grassland and one in subtropical bushveld. Has
**vestigial limbs, long snake-like body with dark
brown and pale yellow longitudinal stripes**.
Length: 570 mm

Warren's girdled lizard
Cordylus warreni, Chakazane
Common and widespread in subtropical bushveld.
Occurs on rocky ridges and outcrops in partly
shaded areas. Two races in Swaziland: one in the
Lebombo range, the other in the central and western parts of the country below 1 000 m. Feeds
on invertebrates especially grasshoppers, beetles
and millipedes. Has **a flattish body with a black
and yellow colour-pattern, square-shaped body
scales and enlarged spiky tail scales**.
Length: 310 mm

Transvaal girdled lizard
Cordylus vittifer, Chakazane
Common and widespread wherever there are narrow, vertical or horizontal rock crevices. Juveniles usually found under stones as adults occupy the best rock cracks. Feeds on invertebrates especially grasshoppers, beetles and millipedes. Live bearing giving birth to 1 to 3 young in early summer. Has **a uniform brown colour with a pale yellow or white stripe down the middle of the back, and enlarged spiky tail scales**.
Length: 180 mm

Drakensberg crag lizard
Pseudocordylus melanotus, Chakazane
Common and widespread in the temperate high-veld region, absent from subtropical bushveld regions. Occurs in montane grassland areas favouring prominent rock outcrops and cliff edges. Often seen basking on a rock pinnacle. Feeds on insects such as grasshoppers and beetles. Adults occupy prime sites and chase others away. Has **a flattened body with a vivid black and orange pattern and enlarged spiky tail scales**.
Length: 280 mm

Common flat lizard
Platysaurus intermedius natalensis
Common and widespread in the central and southern bushveld. Occurs in mountainous terrain with large granite boulders and exposed bedrock. Very agile diurnal lizards. Another species, *P. lemboensis*, is restricted to the Lebombo range. Males are vividly coloured in green, blue, orange and black. Females and juveniles have black and yellow longitudinal stripes. Has **a very flat body, finely beaded body scales and broad head**.
Length: 175 mm

CHELONIANS
Serrated hinged terrapin
Pelusios sinuatus, Lufudvu lwemanti
Common and widespread in bushveld, absent from highveld. Occurs along large perennial rivers and in man-made habitats. Seen basking on logs, rocks or sandbars. Feeds on carrion, fish, amphibians, water plants and wild fruits. The helmeted terrapin, *Pelomedusa subrufa,* prefers temporary pans and borrow pits, avoiding rivers. Has **serrated marginal shields on the hind portion of the shell, a hinging plastron and a large size**.
Length: 400 mm   Mass: 7 kg

Leopard tortoise
Geochelone pardalis, Lufudvu lwesiganga
Common and widespread in subtropical bushveld,
absent from highveld. Occurs in savanna and
bushveld habitats. Its range extends westwards up
the larger river basins (e.g. Komati). One of three
local terrestrial tortoises. Active during and after
summer rain showers. Feeds on a variety of plants
and wild fruits. Has **a pale yellow shell with a
black mottled pattern and no nuchal shield**.
Hardy and thrives in captivity.
Length: 400 mm   Mass: 10 kg

Speke's hinged tortoise
Kinixys spekii, Lufudvu lwesiganga
Common in subtropical bushveld regions, absent
from temperate highveld. Range extends westwards up the larger river basins. One of two local
hinged tortoises. Active during and after summer
rain showers. Shell is pale yellow-brown with or
without a dark radiated pattern. Feeds on plants,
snails, millipedes and other invertebrates. Has **a
hinging hind part of the carapace and upper
jaw with a single beak.**
Length: 200 mm   Mass: 800 g

Natal hinged tortoise
Kinixys natalensis, Lufudvu lwesiganga
Occurs only in eastern subtropical bushveld along
the length of the Lebombo range and foothills.
"Near Threatened" due to habitat loss. Active during and after summer rain. Shell is pale yellow-
brown with or without a dark concentric pattern
on each carapacial shield. Diet similar to previous
species. Has **a poorly defined hinge on the hind
part of the carapace and upper jaw with a tricuspid beak**.
Length: 160 mm   Mass: 650 g

CROCODILES
Nile crocodile
Crocodylus niloticus, Ingwenya
Restricted to the subtropical bushveld. Occurs
primarily in rivers but also in dams and irrigation
canals. Suitable breeding sites are found only in
remote wild areas such as gorges in the Lebombo
mountains. Has been sighted as far west as
Maguga Dam on the Komati River. Categorised
as "Vulnerable" from habitat loss and human
persecution. Feeds on fish, terrapins, birds and
mammals.
Length: 5 m

Invertebrates

Invertebrates encompass a multitude of organisms from microscopic bacteria to fairly large organisms like jellyfish. The more familiar include millipedes, centipedes, snails, crabs, insects, spiders and scorpions. In many cases identification of invertebrates is only possible to family, genus and species level by using technical publications that are not available to the layperson. Consequently, invertebrate groups rather than species are described in this section. There are a few exceptions where a species is distinctive enough to be identified. The class, order and family to which the groups belong are given.

Invertebrates in many cases are the primary consumers in food chains and play a significant role in the transfer of energy from the producers (green plants) to other consumers (animals). Invertebrates are important components of food webs as they provide a source of food to numerous fish, amphibian, reptilian, bird and mammalian predators. Invertebrates are wonderfully diverse in form and in their survival strategies. None of the twelve or so scorpions in Swaziland are dangerous to man. The larger species are very docile and seldom sting whereas the small, more cryptic species sting readily. Stings from these are very painful but not life-threatening. Further reading is recommended on page 170.

PHIL PERRY

Millipedes, Lishongololo

Class *Myriapoda,* Order *Diplopoda*

Widespread and common. Found in moist surroundings usually under cover. Colour variable, some banded. Nocturnal. Feed on plant material softened by decay.

Length: 80 mm

C & M STUART

Centipedes, Inyoka yebafati

Class *Myriapoda,* Order *Chilopoda*

Widespread and common. Found in moist or dry surroundings under cover. Nocturnal. Carnivores that feed on other invertebrates such as insects.

Length: 100 mm

PHIL PERRY

Slugs and snails, Umnenkhe

Class *Gastropoda*

Widespread. Common in highveld. Terrestrial and aquatic. Prefer moist surroundings. Inactive during dry periods. Nocturnal. Feed on vegetable matter. Some are carnivorous.

Length: 100 mm

PAUL LEROY

Freshwater crab, Inkhala

Class *Crustacea,* Order *Decapoda*

Widespread and common. Occurs in rivers and dams. Mostly aquatic but moves overland during wet conditions. Nocturnal. Carnivorous scavengers and hunters.

Length: 80 mm

Dragonflies and damselflies

Class *Insecta*, Order *Odonata*

Occur near rivers, dams and pans. Wings at right angles to (dragonflies) or parallel to (damselflies) body. Colourful. Have aquatic nymphs (larvae). Carnivorous.

Length: 70 mm

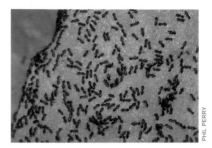

Termites, Emagenge

Class *Insecta*, Order *Isoptera*, Family *Termitidae*

Widespread but more common in highveld. Live in colonies. Mounds dome shaped and free of vegetation (genus *Trinervitermes*). Feed on grass, wood or detritus.

Length: 6 mm

Praying mantids, Mashisindlu

Class *Insecta*, Order *Mantodea*, Family *Mantidae*

Occur in wide range of habitats. Cryptically coloured or shaped. Attracted to lights at night to hunt flying insects. Ambush insect prey using forelegs.

Length: 120 mm

Stick insects, Mashisindlu

Class *Insecta*, Order *Phasmatodea*

Widespread but uncommon. Occur on plant and tree foliage and in grass. Usually immobile and well camouflaged. Move clumsily. Feed on vegetation.

Length: 90 mm

Earwigs, Mkhotsane

Class *Insecta*, Order *Dermaptera*

Widespread and common. Occur under rocks, rotting logs and debris. Nocturnal. Omnivorous. Sometimes capture insect prey using forceps at tip of abdomen.

Length: 24 mm

Armoured ground crickets, Cutfu

Class *Insecta*, Order *Orthoptera*, Family *Bradyporidae*

Widespread. Prefer arid subtropical bushveld. Grasshopper-like with long antennae and a short, stubby body. Found on plants, soil and rock. Mainly herbivorous. Nocturnal.

Length: 30 mm

KATE BRAUN

JOHN LEROY

Locusts, Intsetse

Class *Insecta*, Order *Orthoptera*, Family *Pyrgomorphidae*
Widespread and common. Occur in wide range of habitats. Usually gregarious. Brightly coloured. Only fly when older and can form large swarms. Herbivorous.
Length: 80 mm

Cicadas, Inyekevu

Class *Insecta*, Order *Hemiptera*, Family *Cicadidae*
Widespread and common in bushveld and woodland. Found on tree branches and trunks. Produce loud incessant buzz. Usually heard, seldom seen. Feed on sap. Preyed on by birds.
Length: 40 mm

JOHN LEROY

BOB FORRESTER

Stink bugs

Class *Insecta*, Order *Hemiptera*, Family *Pentatomidae*
Widespread. Occur singly or in groups on plants and trees. Body flattened and shield-like. Produce unpleasant odour when handled. Usually brown or grey. Feed on sap.
Length: 15 mm

Water scorpions

Class *Insecta*, Order *Hemiptera*, Family *Nepidae*
Occur amongst water plants and mud in ponds and slow flowing rivers. Have long tail-like breathing tube. Feed on insects and small aquatic vertebrates (e.g. tadpoles).
Length: 55 mm

JOHN LEROY

NEIL GRAY

Tiger beetles, Libhungane

Class *Insecta*, Order *Coleoptera*, Family *Carabidae*
Widespread and common. Prefer sandy areas. Brightly coloured (genus *Lophyra*) and able to fly. Large eyes with good vision. Fast running diurnal predators. Feed on other insects.
Length: 10 mm to 40 mm

Dung beetles, Libhungane

Class *Insecta*, Order *Coleoptera*, Family *Scarabaeidae*
Occur on the ground near animal dung. Use of dung varies. Some females roll a dung ball, lay one egg in it and bury the ball. After hatching the larva feeds on the dung.
Length: 30 mm

Blister beetles, Libhungane

Class *Insecta*, Order *Coleoptera*, Family *Meloidae*
Occur on foliage of plants and trees. Body elongate with hard wing cases. Usually brightly coloured. Herbivorous. Body contains a drug that can blister the skin.
Length: 40 mm

Spider wasps, Manyovu

Class *Insecta*, Order *Hymenoptera*, Family *Pompilidae*
Body dark with long curled antennae. Females run around on the ground searching for spider prey. Prey is stung and paralysed. A single egg is laid on it and the prey buried.
Length: 35 mm

Hawk moths, Luvivane

Class *Insecta*, Order *Lepidoptera*, Family *Sphingidae*
Large grey or black moths with stout body. Antennae thick, curved and hooked at tip. Forewings long, narrow and forward pointing. Active at dusk and dawn. Feed on honey.
Length: 45 mm

African monarch, Luvivane

Class *Insecta*, Order *Lepidoptera*, Family *Danaidae*
Widespread. Large-winged and brightly coloured (*Danaus chrysippus*). Flies all year. Distasteful to birds because of poisonous chemicals stored in its body.
Wingspan: 70 mm

Citrus swallowtail, Luvivane

Class *Insecta*, Order *Lepidoptera*, Family *Papilionidae*
Widespread. Large-winged and brightly coloured (*Papilio demodocus*). Flies all year. Frequently visits gardens. Larva feeds on various *Citrus*, *Clausena* and *Vepris* plants.
Wingspan: 130 mm

Golden-brown baboon spider

Class *Arachnida*, Order *Araneae*, Family *Theraphosidae*
Widespread. Large robust hairy spider (genus *Pterinochilus*). Lives in silk-lined burrows. Feeds on millipedes and insects ambushed at burrow mouth. Venom not dangerous to man.
Length: 50 mm

Banded-legged golden orb spider

Class *Arachnida*, Order *Araneae*, Family *Tetragnathidae*
Widespread. Large spider with cylindrical abdomen and yellow-banded legs *(Nephila senegalensis)*. Spins large orb web from yellow silk. Feeds on flying insects. Mild venom.
Length: 30 mm

Rain spiders, Bulembu

Class *Arachnida*, Order *Araneae*, Family *Heteropodidae*
Widespread. Large spiders with dark brown markings on abdomen (genus *Palystes*). Live in vegetation. Enter houses. Feed on insects. Preyed on by spider wasps. Mild venom.
Length: 40 mm

Kite spiders, Bulembu

Class *Arachnida*, Order *Araneae*, Family *Araneidae*
Widespread in woodland and forest. Small spiders with a hard body with spiny projections (genus *Gasteracantha*). Construct an orb web under the tree canopy.
Length: 8 mm

Sun spiders, Sayobi

Class *Arachnida*, Order *Solifugae*
Widespread. Medium sized hairy spider-like creatures. Have enormous jaws but lack venom. Active during the day. Feed on insects and other arachnids, including scorpions.
Length: 40 mm

Buthid scorpions, Fecele

Class *Arachnida*, Order *Scorpiones*, Family *Buthidae*
Widespread. Found in trees, rock cracks, under bark and stones. Small, narrow bodied and colourful (genus *Uroplectes*). Run fast with tails straight out. Sting readily.
Length: 25 mm to 50 mm

Liochelid scorpions, Fecele

Class *Arachnida*, Order *Scorpiones*, Family *Liochelidae*
Widespread. Found under rocks, logs and other debris. Medium-sized with a dark grey or black body, one with lighter legs (genus *Opisthacanthus*). Nocturnal. Feed on insects.
Length: 90 mm to 100 mm

Trees

Swaziland has a wealth of tree and shrub species - the country's variety of landscapes, geology and climate result in a corresponding wide range of habitats and biodiversity. In comparison with Mpumalanga and the Kruger National Park (which together have over 950 species of trees and shrubs), Swaziland, which is barely the size of the Kruger Park, boasts more than 700 species. The highest numbers of tree species are found in the Lebombo Mountains in the east of the country, near Lufafa Peak in the northwest and around Sinceni Mountain in central Swaziland. At least 56 of these trees are listed in the Swaziland Plant Red Data Book. Nineteen of these are not found in any protected area. Several endemic tree species are known to be restricted to the Lebombo Mountain range. This highlights the importance of the Lebombos and the need for conservation efforts to adequately protect them.

The following trees are some of the most extensively used in traditional medicines regionally – as a result they are becoming increasingly rare. The bark, stem and roots of *Warburgia salutaris* (pepper-bark tree/ sibhaha) are used for treating coughs and colds. The bark of *Prunus africana* (African almond/ umdumezulu) is used extensively to treat prostate cancer. *Curtisia dentata* (assegai/ lincayi) is not only used for carpentry, the bark treats stomach complaints and it is also used for purifying blood. The fruit of the highly productive *Sclerocarya birrea* (marula/umganu) is used locally and commercially for making jelly, beer and cosmetic products. In this section 72 of the more common and conspicuous trees are featured. Emphasis has been placed on those that one is likely to see travelling along a cross-section of Swaziland from the highveld in the western region to the lowveld and Lebombo mountains in the east.

For further reading, recommended books include Schmidt *et al.* (2002), Pooley (1994) and Coates Palgrave (2002). Loffler and Loffler (2005) presents distribution maps and additional notes for trees and shrubs occurring in the country.

Boscia albitrunca
Shepherd's tree, Siphiso
Small tree with rounded, much branched crown, often with a "browse-line". Occurs in hot, arid bushveld, often associated with termite mounds. Bark **smooth, grey to whitish-grey**. Leaves **greyish-green, side veins barely visible on both surfaces**, often clustered on reduced shoots. Flowers in dense clusters, small, yellowish-green, heavily scented (July-Nov). Fruit a yellowish, round berry. The bark is used to treat vomiting.

CAPPARACEAE Height: up to 7 m

LINDA LOFFLER

B **SB** **L**

Burchellia bubalina
Wild pomegranate, Mahlosana
Shrub or small evergreen tree, occurring in forests, along forest margins, in grassland, often on rocky outcrops. Usually multi-stemmed with a smooth, grey-brown bark. Leaves opposite, **broadly ovate,** glossy dark green. Petiole long, **thickset and hairy**. Flowers very showy in tubular, **dense terminal clusters, scarlet to orange** (Sept-Dec). Fruit urn-shaped, crowned by **persistent calyx lobes**. Roots used as an emetic.

RUBIACEAE Height: up to 8 m

LINDA LOFFLER

G **F**

B L F

Gardenia volkensi subsp. *volkensi*
Bushveld gardenia, Umvalasangweni
A small, rigid tree, often multi-stemmed occurring in bushveld. Bark pale grey, flaking. Leaves opposite or 3-whorled at the end of short, side shoots, obovate to almost triangular, **hairy pits (domatia) present below**. Large, white, showy flowers, sweetly scented turning yellowish with age (Jul-Dec). Fruit almost round, ribbed, grey-green with raised white lumpy dots, about the size of a hen's egg. Believed to ward off evil spirits.
RUBIACEAE Height: up to 10 m

SB G B L

Vangueria infausta
Velvet wild-medlar, Umntulu
Small deciduous tree found in bushveld, wooded grassland and on rocky hillsides. Main stem usually single, grey and smooth, becoming rough and peeling with age. Leaves large, opposite, almost round, **thickly furry,** especially when young. Flowers small, greenish-white in dense clusters, usually below the leaves (Sept-Nov). Fruit edible, green, ripening to yellowish-brown, roundish, smelling like a baked apple when ripe.
RUBIACEAE Height: 2-8 m

F G SB L

Canthium inerme
Turkey-berry, Umvutfwamini
Small tree found in forest, on rocky outcrops and wooded grassland. Main stem single, bark smoothish, pale creamy-grey, young stems branching at right angles with **strong, straight thorns**. Leaves **hairless**, opposite, restricted to new growth at the ends of the branches. Flowers very small, greenish in **many-flowered** axillary heads (Aug-Dec). Fruit edible, oval shaped, glossy green, turning brown when ripe.
RUBIACEAE Height: 2-6 m

SB B L F

Breonadia salicina
Matumi, Umhlume
Medium to very large, evergreen tree, usually along the water's edge **of riverine forests** and **of permanent rivers and streams** at lower altitudes. Main stem tall and straight with a narrow crown. Leaves simple, in whorls of 3 - 5, **long and narrow**, crowded at the ends of the branches, **midrib raised and yellowish**. Flowers small, in compact, round, axillary, pompom-like heads, heavily scented (Nov-Dec). Fruit a small capsule.
RUBIACEAE Height: 3-30 m

Dombeya rotundifolia
Common wild pear, Umwuwane
A shapely, small, deciduous tree widespread especially in bushveld and wooded grassland. Single main stem, crooked, with dark brown, **roughly fissured** bark. Leaves alternate, **almost circular**, thick, **rough like sandpaper** with prominent **net veins** below. Sweetly scented flowers, white to pale pink in axillary clusters blooming before the appearance of new leaves in early spring (Jul-Oct). Fruit a round, silky-haired capsule.
STERCULIACEAE Height: up to 10 m

Pterocelastrus echinatus
White candlewood, Sehlulamanya
Shrub or small tree found in rocky outcrops, grassland and along evergreen forest margins. Main stem grey to pale brown, young stems reddish brown. Leaves alternate, sometimes notched with entire margins, **colour bluish-green.** Young leaves and petiole pink to red. Flowers creamy white in short compact axillary heads (Feb-June). Fruit orange-yellow, 3-lobed capsules, each lobe with **one or more spikes** (Oct-March).
CELASTRACEAE Height: up to 7 m

Maytenus undata
Koko tree, Umbatancwephe
Often a multi-stemmed shrub or small evergreen tree found in bushveld, forest and grassland, often on rocky outcrops. Bark grey-brown, smooth becoming fissured in older specimens. Leaves, alternate, serrated, very variable in size. **Top of leaf blade turning white if folded up**. Flowers in clusters, small, pale yellow to green. Fruit yellow, 3-valved capsules, seeds completely enveloped with a yellow aril. A very variable species.
CELASTRACEAE Height: up to 6 m

Gymnosporia senegalensis
Red spike-thorn, Sihlangu lesimhlophe
A widespread evergreen shrub or small, multi-stemmed tree. Main stem reddish when young, becoming greyish-green. Leaves usually spirally arranged with an evenly serrated margin and a **paler midrib than the rest of the leaf blade**. Flowers creamy white to pale green in dense axillary clusters, often sweetly scented (July-Sept). Fruit a 2-valved capsule, red to pink, seed partially covered with a pink to yellow aril.
CELASTRACEAE Height: up to 15 m

137

LINDA LOFFLER

G · SB · L

Gymnosporia buxifolia
Common spike-thorn, Sihlangu lesimnyama
An evergreen shrub or small tree, widely distributed on rocky outcrops in wooded grassland, bushveld and along rivers. **Bark thick,
dark-brown and rough**, longitudinally fissured.
Leaves in clusters on dwarf, spur branchlets.
Flowers small, whitish in flowerheads in leaf axils
with strong, unpleasant smell (June-March). Fruit
a 3-lobed capsule, brown or reddish, small and
rough with seeds partially covered by **yellow** aril.
CELASTRACEAE Height: usually 3-4 m but up to 9 m

LINDA LOFFLER

SB · L · B

Ficus glumosa
Hairy rock fig, Inkhokhokho
Small to medium-sized tree, often a rock-splitter, found in bushveld and wooded grassland,
usually on rocky hillsides. Bark **cream to yellowish-green**, exfoliating. Branchlets covered in
yellowish-brown hairs. Leaves roundish and alternate, **densely hairy when young**, mature leaves
losing hair on upper surface. Bud sheaths **reddish
brown and papery**. Figs in pairs in the leaf axils,
stalkless and hairy (Jan-Jun) eaten by wildlife.
MORACEAE Height: up to 10 m

LINDA LOFFLER

G · SB · L

Ficus ingens
Red-leaved rock fig, Umkhiwane
Small to medium-sized deciduous tree, commonly
found as a rock-splitter in grassland and bushveld
on rocky terrain. Main stem short and crooked,
smooth, grey to yellowish-grey. Young leaves in
spring strikingly **wine-red to coppery** becoming stiff and dark green with a rounded to heart-
shaped base. Figs, axillary borne in pairs on short
stalks (Jun-Dec), pink or red when ripe, eaten by
birds and animals. Bark used to treat diarrhoea.
MORACEAE Height: up to 18 m

LINDA LOFFLER

SB · G · F · L

Ficus sur
Broom cluster fig, Umkhiwa
Large, spreading, semi-deciduous tree usually
along water courses in woodland and forest. Bark
white when young becoming dark grey with
age, smooth and exuding a **milky latex** when cut.
Leaves alternate with an **irregularly toothed
margin** and a flush of coppery new leaves in
spring. Figs large, orange-red when ripe, **forming
large clusters on the main stem, lower branches and roots**, enjoyed by humans and wildlife.
MORACEAE Height: up to 12 m

Ficus sycomorus
Common cluster fig, Umkhiwa

Large, striking tree, found in bushveld typically in low-lying riverine vegetation. Bark **whitish to yellow-orange, powdery in patches**. Leaves heart-shaped often with a sandpapery upper surface. Figs in heavy, **branched masses on the trunk and main branches**, stalk up to 20mm long. The fruit is edible. Many large individuals were swept away from the river banks during Cyclone Demoina and more recent flood events.

MORACEAE Height: up to 25 m

LINDA LOFFLER

(B) (SB) (L) (F)

Ficus burkei
Common wild fig, Inkhokhokho

A briefly deciduous medium-sized, spreading tree with aerial roots, often a strangler. Found in forest, wooded grassland, commonly on rocky hillsides. Main stem pale to dark grey, smoothish, exuding a **milky latex when cut**. Leaves alternate or whorled, petiole 7-48mm. Figs edible, without stalks in pairs in leaf axils, green with white spots becoming dull red when mature. The roots are used locally as a post-natal supplement.

MORACEAE Height: up to 18 m

LINDA LOFFLER

(G) (F) (SB) (L)

Strychnos madagascariensis
Black monkey-orange, Umkhwakhwa

A small, shrubby, deciduous, multi-stemmed tree, in bushveld, dry rocky areas and low-lying riverine vegetation. Bark pale grey and smooth with **short, rigid lateral shoots**, resembling spines. Leaves opposite, **almost circular** with 3-5 veins from base, clustered towards end of twigs. Flowers small, greenish-yellow in axils of leaves (Oct-Dec). Tennis ball sized fruit, **bluish-green ripening to orange**, with a thick, woody shell.

STRYCHNACEAE Height: up to 8 m

KATE BRAUN

(SB) (B) (L)

Anthocleista grandiflora
Forest fever tree, Umhhobohhobo

Tall, evergreen tree with a straight stem, branching high up, occurring along rivers, in evergreen forest at medium altitude. Swaziland is its southernmost distribution. Bark smooth, pale grey to grey-brown. Leaves are characteristically **very large up to 1.5m x 450mm** and densely clustered at ends of branches. Flowers jasmine scented, in large, branched terminal heads, creamy white (Sept-Jan). Fruit fleshy, oval and green.

GENTIANACEAE Height: up to 20 m

ERNST SCHMIDT

(F) (SB)

LINDA LOFFLER

G F

Greyia sutherlandii
Glossy bottlebrush, Umwatsawatsa
A shrub or small, crooked tree occurring on mountain slopes, forest margins and among rocks in grassland. Bark reddish grey and smooth when young becoming rough with age. Leaves almost succulent, alternate, circular and serrate, **hairless, sticky when young**. Red, showy bell-shaped flowers (Aug-Oct), the nectar attracts birds. Fruit a cylindrical capsule. The wood is soft and used for carving.
GREYIACEAE Height: up to 7 m

LINDA LOFFLER

SB B

Terminalia sericea
Silver cluster-leaf, Sihhomuhhomu
Small to medium-sized deciduous tree usually with a flat-topped crown, in woodland and bushveld, normally on sandy soils. Forms dense stands with characteristic **silvery-grey foliage**. Main stem upright, straight with dark brown or purplish branchlets, **peeling and flaking** in rings and strips. Flowers very small, in axillary spikes in axils of leaves (Sept-Jan). Fruit surrounded by a wing, deep pink to reddish brown. Wood hard.
COMBRETACEAE Height: up to 8 m

LINDA LOFFLER

B SB L

Combretum imberbe
Leadwood, Umphulumbu
Large, deciduous, **greyish**, tree occurring in Acacia nigrescens woodland and bushveld, often near watercourses. Bark pale grey and rough, **cracked in rectangular blocks**. Leaves opposite on **spine-like lateral shoots**, grey-green. Flowers whitish-yellow in axillary **spikes**. Fruit 4-winged, small pale yellowish-green turning brown. Very hard wood. Known to live for hundreds of years, one tree (now dead) estimated at 1,050 years.
COMBRETACEAE Height: up to 20 m

LINDA LOFFLER

F G SB

Combretum kraussii
Forest bushwillow, Imbondvo lemhlophe
Medium to tall mostly evergreen tree with characteristic reddish autumn and **whitish spring** colours. Canopy species associated with evergreen forest, rocky outcrops in grassland and forested ravines. Multi-stemmed with grey to dark grey bark. Leaves opposite and flowers creamy-white in elongated, axillary spikes, borne in dense heads in leaf axils (Aug-Nov). Fruit 4-winged tinged pink to dark red. A good garden subject.
COMBRETACEAE Height: up to 20 m

Combretum molle
Velvet bushwillow, Imbondvo lemnyama

Small to medium-sized deciduous tree widespread in bushveld and woodland often on rocky hillsides. Main stem tall with a greyish-brown, rough and blocky bark. Leaves, opposite, **densely velvety**, with sunken venation giving a **quilted appearance**. Flowers emerge prolifically in dense axillary spikes and are heavily scented, greenish-yellow to yellow (Sept-Nov). Fruit small, 4-winged, yellowish-green becoming red when dry.

COMBRETACEAE Height: up to 9 m

SB · G · B · L

Ilex mitis
Cape holly, Inchitsamuti

Medium to large, evergreen tree with a dense crown, usually along rivers and streams in forests. Bark light brown becoming rough and fissured with age. **Branchlets pale grey to white**, young stems smooth with raised dots. Leaves alternate with **mid-rib sunken above and reddish purple petiole**, apex and base narrowly tapering. Flowers white in dense clusters in leaf axils (Sept-Feb). Fruit a shiny, small, berry.

AQUIFOLIACEAE Height: up to 30 m

F · G · SB

Aloe arborescens
Krantz aloe, Imbovane

Much branched aloe forming a dense shrub-like bush with many rosettes, found on **cliffs, rocky hillsides** and forests in high rainfall areas. Leaves are curved, **dullish grey or bluish green**. Flowers in 3-4 large racemes, **coral-red to salmon-pink** (June-July), attracting many bird species. Decorative garden plant. Leaves used in traditional medicine to treat high blood pressure, diabetes and wounds.

ASPHODELACEAE Height: up to 3 m

G · F · SB · L

Aloe marlothii subsp. marlothii
Mountain aloe, Inhlaba

Single-stemmed, robust aloe, bearded with old, dry leaves for half its length. Widespread in wooded grassland, on rocky hillsides and bushveld, often forming extensive stands. Leaves dull grey-green covered in **sharp hard spines on both surfaces** with reddish-brown teeth along the margins. Flower heads branched, carried **more-or-less horizontally**, turning yellowish-orange with copious nectar (June-Aug).

ASPHODELACEAE Height: up to 6 m

G · SB · B · L

LINDA LOFFLER

Maesa lanceolata
False assegai, Umbhongozi
Straggling shrub or small tree often multi-stemmed occurring in rocky outcrops and grass-land, on streams and river banks. Often a pioneer species. Branches smooth with raised dots and the bark greyish-brown. Leaves alternate, glossy green with **prominent venation below**. Flowers small, white to cream in large branched heads (Nov-Aug). Fruit whitish-pink, round, hanging in dense clusters, reported to be toxic.
MAESACEAE Height: up to 6 m

G SB

LINDA LOFFLER

Ochna natalitia
Natal plane, Mickey Mouse bush, Mahlanganisa
Shrublet or small tree, occurring in bushveld, for-est and grassland, often among rocks and along forest margins. Bark grey-brown becoming rough with age, usually with **galls**. Leaves alternate with secondary veins closely spaced and set at **90 de-grees to the midrib**, young leaves bright red. Flowers large, bright yellow (Sept-Dec). Fruit black, oval drupes surrounded by red to pink sepals.
OCHNACEAE Height: up to 10 m

SB G L F

LINDA LOFFLER

Syzygium cordatum
Waterberry, Umncozi
A medium-sized evergreen tree with a dense, spreading crown, often with a crooked stem. Found along streams and rivers. Main stem tall with a rough, corky bark turning dark grey when mature. **Branchlets 4-angled**. Leaves oppo-site, leathery and often waxy, **with a short stalk**. Flowers creamy-white to pink, fluffy, strong-ly scented in branched terminal heads (Aug-Jan). Fruit an edible berry, deep purple when ripe.
MYRTACEAE Height: up to 15 m

G SB F L

LINDA LOFFLER

Heteropyxis natalensis
Weeping lavender tree, Inkunzi
Small to medium, deciduous tree with **droop-ing** foliage found in bushveld, forests and grass-land, often in rocky places. Main stem single, crooked, **pale grey to almost white, flaking** on all the stems. Leaves narrow, glossy green, with a pleasant **lavender scent when crushed**. Flowers small, yellowish-white in branched terminal clus-ters (Dec-Mar). Fruit small, shiny, brown oval capsules. Flowers attract bees and butterflies.
HETEROPYXIDACEAE Height: up to 10 m

SB G F L

Brachylaena transvaalensis
Forest silver oak, Umphahla

An evergreen, medium to tall tree occurring in and along the margins of forests and wooded grassland. The main stem is usually single, **grey to pale brown**. Leaves **elliptic**, alternate with a **narrowly tapering base**. Flowers in **dense, elongated clusters** (July-Sept). Fruit a small nutlet with creamy-brown bristles. The wood is hard, used for rural homestead construction.

ASTERACEAE Height: up to 25 m

Pterocarpus angolensis
Kiaat, Umvangati

Medium sized deciduous tree with a **flat, spreading crown**, found in bushveld and woodland often on rocky hillsides. Main stem straight and tall with rough, dark grey, blocky bark resembling crocodile skin. Leaves compound, **leaflets in 5-9 sub-opposite pairs**. Flowers yellow, scented, in hanging bunches (Aug-Dec). Pods circular with a **central seed densely covered with coarse bristles, surrounded by a broad thin, wavy wing**.

FABACEAE Height: up to 30 m

Schotia brachypetala
Weeping boerbean, Vovovo

Decorative, medium sized semi-deciduous tree with large, hanging branches found in warm, dry bushveld, along river banks and woodland. Bark rough, grey-brown. Leaves compound, alternate with **4-7 pairs of opposite leaflets**. Leaf stalk sometimes winged. Flowers deep red or scarlet in dense clusters on old wood, **petals reduced to thread-like filaments** (Aug-Nov), Pods are woody, dark brown and flat, splitting on the tree.

FABACEAE Height: up to 16 m

Englerophytum magalismontanum
Transvaal milk plum, Umnumbela

Small to medium-sized evergreen tree with a rounded, densely leafy crown. Main stem short, crooked, grey and smooth, **with visible scars on branches from fallen fruit**. Leaves alternate, often crowded near the ends of branches, **densely covered with reddish-brown to silvery hairs below**. Flowers small, strong smelling in compact clusters, brownish pink (Jun-Dec). Fruit an edible berry **borne in dense clusters on old branches**.

SAPOTACEAE Height: up to 4 m

Erythrina latissima
Broad-leaved coral tree, Siphama

Thickset small to medium deciduous tree with a spreading, rounded crown. Bark very **rough, grey and corky** with scattered thorns on young branches. Leaves 3-foliate, very **large, greyish-green** and leathery, **densely covered with woolly hairs when young.** Flowers in compact flower heads, crimson to brownish-red (Aug-Sept). Fruit large cylindrical pods, constricted between the seeds. Seeds orange to red with a black spot.

FABACEAE Height: up to 12 m

Erythrina lysistemon
Sacred coral tree, Umsinsi

Striking small to medium deciduous tree found on wooded mountainsides, in bushveld, and along forest fringes. Broad trunk branching from low down. Bark grey and smooth, often with scattered thorns. Leaves 3-foliate with heart-shaped leaflets and **two long glands at their base.** Flowers showy, bright red (Jun-Oct). Fruit a slender cylindrical pod, **bead-like.** Poisonous red seeds, ornamental with a black spot, known as lucky beans.

FABACEAE Height: up to 12 m

Phoenix reclinata
Wild date palm, Lisundvu

Multi-stemmed palm growing in **dense clumps** along watercourses and in open grassland. The stems are slender and often reclining. Leaves **feather-shaped** and crowded at the top of the stems with **arching fronds.** Sexes separate on different trees. Male flowers in bunches of pollen-laden creamy, white flowers (Aug-Oct). Edible fruit bright **orange to brownish** in large, hanging bunches. Sap sometimes tapped for wine.

ARECACEAE Height: up to 10 m

Celtis africana
White stinkwood, Unvumvu

Deciduous tree found in forests, riverine vegetation and wooded grassland. Main stem pale grey to almost whitish, smooth, **young branches hairy.** Leaves alternate, **3-veined from asymmetrical base, serrated margin in upper half,** with a **long tip.** Flowers small, greenish and inconspicuous, sexes separate but both occur on same tree (Aug-Oct). Fruit a yellow drupe on **a long stalk.** Roots and bark used as aphrodisiac.

CELTIDACEAE Height: up to 30 m

Trema orientalis
Pigeonwood, Umbalakancane

Common deciduous tree or shrub occurring in a variety of habitats. Bark smooth, grey with raised white dots and **slightly ascending to horizontal side branches**. Leaves alternate, 3-veined from **rounded to heart-shaped** base, similar to *Celtis africana* but with bigger **serrations** along the margins. Flowers small yellowish-green, sexes separate but both occur on same tree (Sept-Mar). Fruit small, round, black, in bunches.

CELTIDACEAE Height: up to 12 m

SB L F

Diospyros whyteana
Bladdernut, Santinyana

Evergreen shrub or small tree occurring on rocky outcrops, in grassland, forests and riverine bush. Densely branched with smooth bark, **grey to almost black**. Leaves alternate, strikingly dark, glossy green above, wavy, with **densely hairy margins**. Flowers white, sometimes pendulous (Aug-Nov). Fruit a distinctive **inflated, papery calyx** with a bladder-like structure ripening to reddish brown. Roots used to treat wounds.

EBENACEAE Height: up to 7 m

G F SB

Euclea crispa
Escarpment guarri

A much-branched, variable, evergreen shrub or small tree, often forming dense stands. Stems crooked, covered in minute **rusty glands** when young. Bark pale grey to brownish-grey. Leaves opposite, variable, **dull, dark olive-green** above, with a papery texture. Flowers small, greenish-yellow and drooping in **unbranched** sprays, sweetly scented (Dec-May). Fruit edible, round, thinly fleshy, reddish-brown becoming black.

EBENACEAE Height: up to 7 m

SB G B L

Euclea divinorum
Magic guarri, Indlelanyamatane-lebovu

Shrub or small evergreen tree occurring in bushveld, woodland and low-lying riverine vegetation. Multi-stemmed, bark grey and smooth, becoming darker and rougher with age. Leaves opposite, dark green to greyish green, **margin conspicuously wavy**. Flowers very small, white to cream-yellow in short, dense, branched heads (Jul-Jan). Fruit edible, round, thinly fleshy, purplish-black when ripe.

EBENACEAE Height: up to 6 m

B SB

145

LINDA LOFFLER

B SB L

Pappea capensis
Jacket-plum, Liletsa

Small to medium-sized deciduous tree with a dense crown, found in bushveld, woodland and riverine vegetation. Bark grey and smooth with typical white patches. Leaves alternate, variable, leathery and rough with **raised yellow venation** below, often crowded near end of branches. Flowers small, pale green and scented with spike-like heads (Sep-Mar). Fruit in **furry-green** clusters containing **red jelly-covered black seeds**.

SAPINDACEAE Height: up to 13 m

LINDA LOFFLER

B SB L

Acacia nigrescens
Knobthorn, Umkhaya

Tall, handsome, deciduous tree, standing bare for several months in the year. Often associated with Marula trees. The bark is yellowish brown with conspicuous **knobbly prickles**, particularly in young trees. Thorns in **hooked pairs below the node**. Leaves are twice compound, large with **1 or 2 pairs of leaflets**. Flowers are **elongated spikes**, yellowish white and the fruit is flat and straight, darkish brown in colour.

FABACEAE Height: up to 30 m

LINDA LOFFLER

SB B L

Acacia nilotica subsp. *kraussiana*
Scented-pod thorn, Sitfwetfwe

Small to medium-sized thorny tree, often with a mushroom-shaped crown. Typically grows in dense stands in bushveld on poorly drained soils. The bark is black and deeply fissured. Paired thorns are white and usually curved backwards. Leaves twice compound and leaflets small. Flowers are bright, yellow balls (Sep-Apr). Pods are long and **distinctly "beaded", smelling of granadilla** when young.

FABACEAE Height: up to 10 m

LINDA LOFFLER

B SB L F

Acacia robusta subsp. *clavigera*
Brack thorn, Umgamba

Robust, single-stemmed, small to medium-sized tree with rounded crown, usually found at low altitudes along drainage lines and river banks. The bark is rough and grey to dark brown. Thorns paired and **straight, white, joined at base**. Leaves twice compound, **narrow, with hairy leaf axis**. Flowers **creamy-white balls** (Aug-Oct), flowering trees attract honey bees and butterflies. Slightly sickle-shaped pods, grey to dark brown.

FABACEAE Height: up to 20 m

Acacia tortilis subsp. *heteracantha*
Umbrella Thorn, Sitfwetfwe

Distinctive thorny **flat-topped tree,** wide-spread in the eastern and central bushveld. Single stemmed with a rough grey-black bark. Thorns in pairs at nodes, **short and hooked, mixed with long straight ones.** Leaves very small, twice compound, grouped at nodes and sometimes deciduous. Flowers grow in clusters of creamy-white balls (Oct-Feb). Pods are spirally twisted, highly nutritious and browsed by game and stock.

FABACEAE Height: up to 15 m

Acacia xanthophloea
Fever tree, Unkhanyakudze

Large, semi-deciduous tree usually occurring in groups in low-lying areas next to water and on alluvial soils. **The bark is a distinct lime green,** smooth and powdery. Thorns are **straight, white** and paired. Leaves twice compound. Flowers form clusters of golden, yellow balls (Aug-Nov). Smallish pods, straight, narrow and brown. These trees were associated with malaria and fever, sharing a similar habitat to mosquitoes.

FABACEAE Height: up to 30 m

Acacia ataxacantha
Flame thorn, Lugagane

Thorny, scrambling, deciduous, climber often forming impenetrable thickets in riverine vegetation, grassland and bushveld. The bark is light brown and rough and the thorns **single, hooked** and scattered along the branches. Leaves are alternate, twice compound with small leaflets. Flowers are long, **yellowish-white spikes** (Sept-Feb). Young pods are a deep wine-red forming eye-catching patches in the bush.

FABACEAE Height: up to 10 m

Cussonia spicata
Cabbage-tree, Unsenge

Small to medium, deciduous tree with a much-branched rounded crown, usually in rocky outcrops and grasslands, on forest margins and on mountain slopes. Bark grey, thick and corky. Leaves clustered at the ends of branches, twice compound, **subdivided by deep lobes** to the midrib. Flowers densely packed in terminal **double umbels** forming a candelabra-like head (Nov-May). Fruit purple, small, clustered on spikes.

ARALIACEAE Height: up to 18 m

147

Schefflera umbellifera
False cabbage-tree, Umsengembuti
Medium to large evergreen tree with a tall trunk and rounded crown. Usually found in moist forest and along forest margins. Bark rough, greyish brown and longitudinally fissured. Leaves digitate, **very wavy**, clustered at end of branches with 3-5 leaflets spirally arranged. Flowers small, pale yellow to white in **large, branched terminal heads** (Jan-May). Fruit small, round in loose clusters, turning dark red when ripe.
ARALIACEAE Height: up to 20 m

Annona senegalensis subsp. senegalensis
Wild custard-apple, Umtelemba
Shrub or small deciduous tree usually on sandy soils or along rivers. Bark grey with circular flakes exposing patches of paler underbark. **Leaves large, oval to almost circular, apex and base rounded.** Flowers axillary, cream to yellow (Aug-Dec). Fruit edible, large and fleshy, dark green with white spots, tasting similar to custard apple. The tree is often confused with the exotic guava (*Psidium guajava*).
ANNONACEAE Height: up to 5 m

Ziziphus mucronata
Buffalo-thorn, Umlahlabantfu
Small to medium sized tree occurring over most of Swaziland but mainly in bushveld, often on alluvial soils. Main stem crooked, grey to dark grey, roughly fissured. **Thorns in pairs, one straight, one hooked** at each node. Leaves are glossy dark green, alternate, base **markedly asymmetric**. Flowers small, yellowish, in cluster in leaf axils (Oct-Jan). Fruit a reddish-brown berry, often remaining on the tree throughout winter.
RHAMNACEAE Height: up to 12 m

Clerodendrum glabrum
White cat's whiskers, Umphehlacwatsi
Small to medium size deciduous tree with a drooping crown occurring in bushveld, among rocks in grassland, riverine vegetation and on rocky hillsides. Main stem upright branching high up, pale greyish-brown, branches covered in **pale raised whitish dots**. Leaves 3-6 whorled, giving an **unpleasant smell when crushed**. Flowers white, in **dense terminal heads,** attracting insects (Dec-Jun). Fruit yellowish-white, fleshy.
LAMIACEAE Height: up to 10 m

Philenoptera violacea
Apple-leaf, Sihomuhomu

Tall, semi deciduous tree, widespread in the north east in bushveld and along riverine fringes, often on alluvial soils. Bark light grey exuding a red, sticky sap when cut. Leaves compound, **1-3 pairs of leaflets**, large, **greyish-green below**. Flowers violet, **pea-shaped**, in large drooping sprays (Oct-Nov). Pods flat, greyish brown with ridge on one side. Also known as 'rain tree' from spit bugs which suck tree sap and excrete watery droplets.

FABACEAE Height: up to 18 m

SB B

Dichrostachys cinerea subsp. africana
Small-leaved sickle bush, Lusekwane

Multi stemmed, deciduous shrub or acacia-like tree found in bushveld, wooded grassland and grassland. Forms impenetrable thickets in over-grazed and mismanaged areas. Bark light brown, rough, the stems often twisted and branches inter-twined. Twigs modified to form unpaired spines. Leaves twice compound, with **4-9 pairs of pin-nae**. Flowers in elongated pendulous spikes, **pink and yellow** (Oct-Jan). **Pods curly and twisted**.

FABACEAE Height: up to 7 m

B SB L G

Cyathea dregei
Grassland tree fern, Inkhomankhoma

The most common tree fern occurring along mountain streams and seepage areas in grassland, on the margins of evergreen forests and in forest-ed ravines. Stem, erect, usually unbranched, ro-bust and resistant to fire. Leaves arching, up to 3 meters long with **round brown sori in two rows on each lobe**. New fronds appear in spring and is commonly mistaken for a cycad or palm. Exploited by gardeners and now protected by law.

CYATHEACEAE Height: up to 5 m

G F

Euphorbia ingens
Common tree euphorbia, Unhlonhlo, Ishupa

Spiny succulent tree with a short stem and a mas-sive, many branched dark green crown, occurring in medium to low altitude bushveld and wood-ed grassland, often on rocky outcrops. Branchlets **4-5 angled**, irregularly constricted, forming seg-ments with parallel sides. Flowers in clusters, yellowy-green (Apr-Jul). Fruit a round 3-lobed capsule, smooth, reddish. The sap is toxic and used to poison fish.

EUPHORBIACEAE Height: up to 12 m

SB B

SB L F

Antidesma venosum
Tassel berry, Umhlala-mahuhulu
Shrub or small tree, found in bushveld, along rivers and on forest margins. Main stem usually twisted branching low down with a grey to grey-brown, flaky bark. Leaves alternate, glossy bright green above with lateral veins **looping around the margin**. Flowers greenish-yellow, in single or branched flower heads, with an unpleasant smell (Oct-Jan). Fruit edible, round fleshy berries on long pendulous spikes, purplish-black when ripe.
EUPHORBIACEAE Height: up to 8 m

B L

Spirostachys africana
Tamboti, Umtfombotsi
Medium-sized deciduous tree with distinctive **yellow or reddish** autumn colours. Often forms dense stands in low-altitude bushveld. Bark dark grey to blackish, cracking in **rectangular blocks** with a thick **white, poisonous sap**. Leaves alternate, small with a **scalloped margin**. Flowers in pinkish-red spikes appearing before the leaves (Aug-Oct). Fruit a 3-lobed capsule, yellowish-brown, splitting explosively. Wood smoke poisonous.
EUPHORBIACEAE Height: up to 15 m

SB F

Bridelia micrantha
Mitzeeri, Umhlala-magcwababa
Fast growing and shady medium to tall deciduous tree. Occurs in riverine vegetation, forest and open woodland. Main stem straight with dense, spreading crown, bark greyish-brown and rough, often with white patches. Leaves alternate, **turning bright orange in autumn**, veins with 'herringbone' pattern running to the margin**. Flowers yellowish-green, in small clusters in leaf axils (Aug-Oct). Fruit a black, edible, oval berry.
EUPHORBIACEAE Height: up to 20 m

B F

Kigelia africana
Sausage tree, Umvongotsi
Medium to large deciduous tree found in low-lying riverine vegetation and bushveld. Main stem straight with rounded crown. Bark fairly smooth, grey to grey-brown. Leaves compound with 2-5 pairs of leaflets and one terminal leaflet. Flowers large, trumpet-shaped, very dark red, unpleasant smelling (July-Oct). **Very large fruit** (500 x 100mm), **unusual sausage-shaped**, heavy, up to 7kg, **hanging down** on long, stalks (Nov-Aug).
BIGNONIACEAE Height: up to 15 m

Balanites maughamii
Green-thorn, Umnulu
Tall deciduous tree with a **distinctly fluted trunk**
found in dry bushveld, often along river banks.
Branchlets grey-green and hairy, zig-zagged,
spines usually forked. Leaves alternate, compound with only two leaflets, often velvety, hairy
and with short stalks. Flowers green and small in
clusters in leaf axils (July-Nov). Fruit pale yellow-brown, five-grooved at the base turning yellowish when ripe.
BALANITACEAE Height: up to 25 m

Faurea rochetiana
Broad-leaved beechwood, Sicalaba
Small to medium sized deciduous tree occurring
on grassy hillsides, open bushveld and along forest margins. Main stem crooked, dark grey and
deeply furrowed. Leaves, **wavy**, large, alternate,
densely covered with **greyish velvety hairs** below turning **red** in autumn. Flowers in **pendulous
whitish pink spikes** resembling a 'pussycat tail'
turning brown with age (Mar-Sep). Fruit a small
nut, ripening in winter.
PROTEACEAE Height: up to 7 m

Protea roupelliae subsp. roupelliae
Silver protea, Sidlungu
Occurs on rocky mountainsides in high-altitude
grassland. The main stem is single, gnarled, short,
with a thick, black, fissured bark. Leaves curve
upwards in rosettes at the end of branches, **densely covered in silvery hairs** when young. Flower
heads large goblet-shaped with brownish outer
bracts and **spoon-shaped** inner bracts, deep pink,
edged with silvery hairs, flowering all year but
mainly Feb-Apr. Fruit a hairy nutlet.
PROTEACEAE Height: up to 8 m

Sclerocarya birrea subsp. caffra
Marula, Umganu
Medium to large deciduous tree with an erect
trunk and rounded crown. Occurs at medium
to low altitude. Bark grey, rough and flaking in
patches. **Branchlets and twigs rounded and
thick-tipped**. Leaves once compound, alternate
with **slightly asymmetrical base, 3-7 pairs plus
terminal leaflet**. Flowers, small, pink and white
with sexes on separate trees (Sept-Nov). Round,
yellow fruit used in jelly, beer and cosmetics.
ANACARDIACEAE Height: up to 18 m

151

LINDA LOFFLER

G L SB F

Rhus chirindensis
Red currant, Inhlangushane lenkhulu
Medium to large evergreen or deciduous, single-stemmed tree, found in forests and along streams. Bark smooth, brown with **young stems and coppice growth sometimes spiny.** Leaves 3-foliate with **large terminal leaflets**, apex tapering to a sharp tip. **Petiole up to 80mm long** and pinkish. Flowers minute, in axillary and terminal heads (Nov-Mar). Fruit spherical and borne in heavy bunches. Largest *Rhus* species in South Africa.
ANACARDIACEAE Height: up to 20 m

LINDA LOFFLER

B L

Grewia hexamita
Giant raisin, Umsiphane
Large shrub or small deciduous tree, occurs in bushveld and along river valleys. Main stem short and crooked with a rough, dark grey bark and reddish-brown branches. Leaves alternate, **hairless and dark glossy green** above with thick velvety white hairs beneath, prominent venation, asymmetrical base. Flowers showy, honey scented, golden yellow in leaf axils (Sep-Dec). Fruit large, 2-lobed, yellow to red brown.
TILIACEAE Height: up to 5 m

LINDA LOFFLER

SB B F L

Trichilia emetica
Natal mahogany, Umkhuhlu
Medium to large evergreen tree with a **dense spreading crown**, often near water. Bark dark grey-brown, sometimes blocky. Leaves compound with 3-5 pairs of **oblong leaflets, dark glossy green above**. Flowers scented, velvety, creamy-green, in dense flower heads (Aug-Oct). Fruit a creamy-brown, spherical woody capsule splitting into 2-3 valves, with a long neck joined to the stalk. Seed black, covered by a **red aril**.
MELIACEAE Height: up to 25 m

LINDA LOFFLER

B SB L

Carissa bispinosa subsp. *bispinosa*
Common num-num, Umvusankunzi
Spiny, scrambling shrub, usually multi-stemmed, often in hot, dry areas. Bark grey to green and branchlets green, exuding a white latex. Spines opposite, Y-shaped, **robust, forked or twice-forked**. Leaves opposite, thickly leathery. Flowers small, white to pinkish in terminal clusters on short stalks (Aug-Jan). Fruit is edible, red, oval and fleshy. Roots used medicinally. Decorative garden shrub.
APOCYNACEAE Height: up to 3 m

Flowers

This section provides just a glimpse at the amazing variety of wild flowers in Swaziland. The flora checklist for Swaziland includes 3 678 taxa, 3 000 are predominantly small shrubs, herbs and grasses. Grasslands and in particular parts of the Malolotja Nature Reserve, have truly spectacular shows of colour in early spring. There are over a dozen plants endemic to Swaziland as well as a number that occur only in the country and adjacent areas of South Africa and Mozambique. For further reading and identification, recommended books include Pooley (1998) and Van Wyk & Malan (1997). The Swaziland National Trust Commission has an online plant database, www.sntc.org.sz/flora/.

There are very real threats to the survival of viable populations of many flower species and their habitats. These include: the conversion of grasslands to timber plantations, expanding monocultures (like sugar) and rapid urbanisation. Many of these species are used for traditional medicine or are edible and are being harvested at an alarming rate from the wild. The medicinal plant trade is very active in Swaziland; large quantities of indigenous plants, for example various *Aloe* and *Hypoxis* species, are traded within the country as well as illegally across the borders, having a significant negative impact on wild populations.

LINDA LOFFLER

Abrus precatorius
Luckybean creeper, Umphitsi
Deciduous climber found in dry woodland. More than 10 pairs of pinnate leaves with lilac flowers in terminal sprays (Sep-Apr). Pods with **red and black** "lucky-bean", toxic **seeds**.
FABACEAE

LINDA LOFFLER

Adenium multiflorum
Impala lily, Sisilasemphala
Succulent bushveld shrub. Stems and rootstock swollen with poisonous sap. Flowers white lobes with crinkly, **red margins and red stripes** in the throat (May-Sep).
APOCYNACEAE Height: up to 1.5 m

KATE BRAUN

Alepidea amatymbica
Giant alepidea, Inkatsankatsa
Robust herb with large rootstock, found in grassland. Leaves **not in basal rosette**, toothed with bristle tip. Flowers white, star-shaped with **5 unequal bracts** (Jan-Apr).
APIACEAE Height: up to 2 m

PHIL PERRY

Aloe cooperi
Cooper's aloe, Lisheshelu
Solitary, found in open grassland often wedged between rocks. Leaves **fan-shaped, keeled**, whitish spots near base. Inflorescence greenish cream to salmon pink (Dec-Feb).
ASPHODELACEAE Height: up 1.2 m

Aloe suprafoliata
Book aloe, Inhlaba
Solitary, found on rocky mountainsides. Leaves **greyish or bluish-green** in a **flat fan** when young, maturing into a **rosette.** Inflorescence **unbranched**, pink to scarlet (May-Jun).
ASPHODELACEAE Height: up to 1 m

Ansellia africana
Leopard orchid, Liphakama
Epiphytic orchid, **forming large clump**s in upper branches of bushveld forest trees. Leaves alternate, stiff, with parallel veins. Branching flowers yellow with large, dark spots (Jun-Nov).
ORCHIDACEAE Height: up to 1.8 m

Becium obovatum
Cat's whiskers
Velvety shrublet found on mountain grassland. Stems are ribbed, leaves oval and hairy. Flowers in a compact inflorescence, white to pinky-mauve with a **frilly upper lip** (Sept-Feb).
LAMIACEAE Height: up to 300 mm

Boophone distichia
Fan-leaved boophone, Incumbe.
Perennial 'tumbleweed' found in rocky grassland, with part of bulb exposed above ground. Leaves opposite, spread out like an **open fan.** Inflorescence, **spherical pink** (Sept-Nov).
AMARYLLIDACEAE Height: up to 450 mm.

Brunsvigia radulosa
Candelabra flower, Lilula
Solitary 'tumbleweed' found in open rocky grassland. Leaves broad, **rough, spreading flat on the ground**. Striking, large pink flowers (Jan-Feb) borne on a stout peduncle.
AMARYLLIDACEAE Height: up 800 mm

Clematis brachiata
Traveller's joy, Litinyo-lemamba
Perennial woody vine found in woodland, forest margins and on rocky hillsides. Masses of fragrant, creamy white flowers (Feb-Jun). **3-7 leaflets**. Fruit round with long **feathery styles**.
RANUNCULACEAE

GINA JC WILGENBUS

LINDA LOFFLER

Clivia miniata
Clivia, Umayime

Perennial, evergreen lily found on shady forest floors. Red to orange **trumpet-shaped flowers** (Aug-Oct). Leaves pointed to tapering, bases overlapping. Fruit a fleshy red berry.

AMARYLLIDACEAE Height: up to 500 mm

Crocosmia paniculata
Falling stars, Umlunge

Herb found in dense clumps in grassland and rocky outcrops. Tubular inflorescence, yellow-orange, in clusters on **zig-zag branches** (Dec-Feb). Leaves long and broad, **pleated.**

IRIDACEAE Height: up to 2.4 m

LINDA LOFFLER

LINDA LOFFLER

Disa nervosa

Summer-flowering orchid growing in open grassland. Dense cylindrical flowers, bright pink, sometimes with purple spots, **horizontal spur up to 20mm long** (Dec-Mar). Leaves narrow, clasping the stem.

ORCHIDACEAE Height: up to 800 mm

Erica drakensbergensis
Drakensberg heath

Woody shrub growing in rocky grassland and along forest margins. Stem often twisted with **short hairs.** Fluorescence profuse, tiny white bells, **anthers brown** (Aug-Jan).

ERICACEAE Height: up to 2 m

JAMES CULVERWELL

KATE BRAUN

Eucomis autumnalis
Common pineapple flower

Perennial bulb found in grassland. Inflorescence **densely packed** with a **tuft of green, leaf-like bracts**. Flowers white to pale yellow-green (Dec-Apr). Leaves broad with **wavy margins**.

HYACINTHACEAE Height: up to 500 mm

Gladiolus crassifolius
Thick-leaved gladiolus, Sidvwana

Erect herb growing in groups in grassland. Flowers in 2 rows **turned in one direction**, pinkish-white (all year). Leaves stiff, leathery, with a **raised yellow margin and midrib.**

IRIDACEAE Height: up to 1 m

Gloriosa superba
Flame lily, Simiselo.
Lowveld climber found in rocks and thickets. Pendant flowers, bright yellow or flame-coloured, narrow wavy **tepals** (Nov-Mar). Leaves shiny, **tendrils at tips**. **Poisonous**.
FLAGELLARIACEAE Height: up to 2 m

Gnidia caffra
Gnidia, Umshanyelo
Shrublet found in grassland, on rocky outcrops. Conspicuous after veld fires. Flowers lemon yellow, in loose many-flowered terminal heads (Aug-Jan). Leaves **sparsely hairy**.
THYMELAEACEAE Height: up to 1 m

Hypoxis hemerocallidea
Star-flower, Iboya
Perennial herb with fleshy rootstock, found in open grassland and woodland. Flowers yellow, closing at midday (Aug-Apr). Leaves arranged in **3 ranks**, arching outwards.
HYPOXIDACEAE Height: up to 400 mm

Jasminum multipartitum
Common jasmine
Scrambling shrub found in woodland and thicket. Flowers white, **solitary**, strongly scented with up to **11 petal lobes** (Aug-Jan). Leaves **simple**, hairless. Fruit a twin berry shiny black.
OLEACEAE Height: up to 3 m

Leucospermum gerrardii
Soapstone pincushion
Dwarf shrub with underground stems found in rocky grassland. Flowers in round, woolly heads, pinkish-yellow to scarlet-orange (Sept-Nov). Leaves linear with 1-4 glandular teeth.
PROTEACEAE Height: up to 400 mm

Pentanisia prunelloides
Broad-leaved pentanisia, Umgwamiso
Perennial herb found in grassland. Flowers borne in compact almost spherical heads, pale to deep purplish-blue (Oct-Mar). Stems and leaves hairy, leaves simple and opposite.
RUBIACEAE Height: up to 600 mm

Pseudarthria hookeri
Velvet bean
Deciduous woody shrub found in long grass-
land and bushveld. Leaves 3-foliate, **velvety**.
Flowers **pink** in terminal stalk (Sept-Jun). Pods
velvety-mauve, **sticky**. Stems **angular, hairy**.
FABACEAE Height: up to 3 m

Sansevieria hyacinthoides
Mother-in-law's-tongue, Sitfotfokotfo
Rhizomatous herb, seen in colonies in thicket
and woodland. Flowers in **clusters**, greenish-
white to pale mauve, open at night (Sept-May).
Leaves mottled, fibrous. Fruit an orange berry.
DRACAENACEAE Height: up to 600 mm

Scadoxus multiflorus subsp. multiflorus
Fire-ball lily
Deciduous bulb found in bushveld and grass-
land. Round inflorescence, reddish-pink
(Oct-Dec). Leaves shiny with wavy margins,
produced after or with flowers. Fruit a red berry.
AMARYLLIDACEAE Height: up to 1 m

Tecoma capensis
Cape honeysuckle, Malangula
Scrambling shrub found in thicket and on for-
est margins. Terminal flowers orange-red, (all
year), visited by sun-birds, butterflies and bees.
Leaves compound with 2-4 pairs of leaflets.
BIGNONIACEAE Height: up to 4 m

Watsonia densiflora
Natal watsonia, Sidvwa
Tall perennial herb in clumps in grassland.
Stems covered with **brown** fibres. Flowers in
dense spikes, pink (Nov-June). Leaves stiff,
grey-green, with yellow midrib and margin.
IRIDACEAE Height: up to 1.2 m

Xerophyta retinervis
Monkey's tail, Sifunti
Deciduous perennial often on granite outcrops.
Fibrous stems form a fire-proof layer of old
leaf bases. Flowers pale mauve or white (Sept-
Nov, especially after fire). Leaves grasslike.
VELLOZIACEAE Height: up to 1.8 m

NATIONAL PARKS AND RESERVES

HLANE ROYAL NATIONAL PARK

This is the largest protected area in the Kingdom, just under 20 000 hectares of bushveld. Hlane is predominantly *Acacia nigrescens* (knobthorn) woodland with large stands of *Spirostachys africana* (tamboti) and impressive riverine vegetation along several drainage lines. The reserve offers an extensive network of roads linking two camps, waterholes and other features and has camping facilities and self-catering lodges. The roads are passable for two-wheel drive vehicles except after heavy rains. Visitors may walk unescorted near the overnight camps, but need guides for longer walks. Visitors may get out of their vehicles at the Mahlindza waterhole and the Lusoti dam to watch game coming to drink from the comfort of a viewing area. The weather is hot and humid in summer but cooler in winter. One would expect to see around 100 species of birds in a day during spring and early summer. Many large mammal species may be seen here and it has the highest concentration of raptors in the country. Bush encroachment is a problem and elephants have destroyed many trees in certain zones of the park. However there are more pristine areas of hardwood vegetation with mature trees and savannah grassland. The reserve is in a malarial area, therefore precautions need to be taken.

Ideal for viewing
• Marabou stork, martial eagle, African crowned eagle, black sparrowhawk, bateleur, white-headed vulture, crested guineafowl, African finfoot, eastern nicator, bearded scrub-robin, pink-throated twinspot, white-backed night-heron.
• White rhinoceros, elephant, lion, giraffe, kudu.
• Foam nest tree frog, brown-backed tree frog, bubbling kassina, painted reed frog.
• Leopard tortoise, Speke's hinged tortoise, Wahlberg's velvet gecko, southern tree agama, common striped skink, rock monitor, Mozambique spitting cobra, southern African python, Nile crocodile.

HLANE ROYAL NATIONAL PARK, SQUARE-LIPPED RHINOS WITH RED-BILLED OXPECKERS

Map showing the location of some of the reserves and parks, larger cities and towns, main roads and border posts within Swaziland.

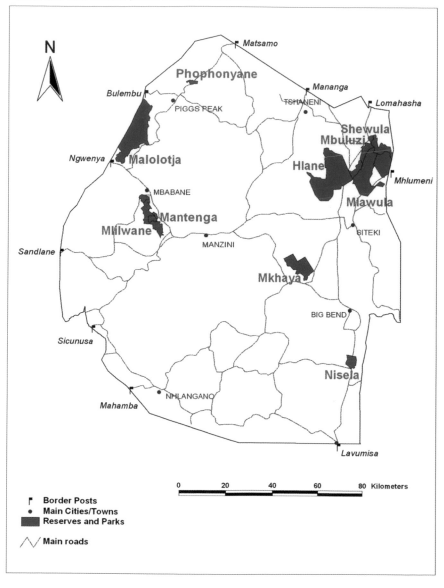

• *Adenium swazicum* (summer impala lily), *Crinum delagoense* (candy-striped crinum) *Combretum imberbe* (leadwood), *Sclerocarya birrea* (marula), *Ansellia africana* (leopard orchid).

MALOLOTJA NATURE RESERVE

This reserve of 18 000 hectares is arguably Swaziland's most attractive, it lies on the edge of the dramatic Drakensberg Escarpment. There are spectacular views of deep plunging gorges and valleys, towering cliffs and numerous waterfalls. The reserve has a wide variety of habitats ranging from above 1 800 m (Ngwenya Mountain) to around 600 m (Komati Valley). The ancient Barberton Greenstone Belt provides a dramatic landscape with montane grassland covering much of the reserve. Mistbelt and riverine forests, gorges, rocky slopes and wetlands in the form of vleis and dams are interesting habitats in the reserve. The bird list of over 280 species is correspondingly diverse, but expect to see around 80 species in a day in spring and early summer. Malolotja is home to one of southern Africa's rarest birds, the magnificent blue swallow. The climate is more temperate than subtropical: summers are generally warm and wet, winters are cool and at night temperatures often drop below freezing. The montane grassland is accessible by car, other interesting habitats can only be reached by walking. Visitors can stay in furnished, equipped log cabins or camp.

Ideal for viewing
• Southern bald ibis, striped flufftail, Denham's bustard, black-winged lapwing, Knysna turaco, ground woodpecker, blue swallow, buff-streaked chat, chorister robin-chat, broad-tailed warbler, white-starred robin, Gurney's sugarbird, African grass-owl, jackal buzzard, black-shouldered kite, secretarybird.
• Eland, blesbok, grey rhebok, mountain reedbuck, common reedbuck, oribi, red hartebeest, aardwolf, serval.
• Guttural toad, raucous toad, striped stream frog, long-toed running frog, painted reed frog.

- Montane specked skink, Distant's ground agama, Cape grass lizard, Drakensberg crag lizard, Nile monitor, olive house snake, common slug eater, short-snouted grass snake, rinkhals.
- *Encephalartos paucidentatus* (Barberton cycad) and *E. laevifolius* (Kaapsehoop cycad), *Podocarpus latifolius* (Broad-leaved yellowwood), *Anthocleista grandiflora* (forest fever tree), *Hemizygia thorncroftii, Agapanthus inapertus* (Drakensburg agapanthus). Six species of *Protea* including *Leucospermum gerrardii* (pincushion protea) and four species of *Erica* (heaths). Numerous species of amaryllids, orchids and lilies and the rock-loving *Streptocarpus dunnii*.

MBULUZI GAME RESERVE

This small reserve of 2 400 hectares lies tucked against the foothills of the Lebombo mountains in north-eastern Swaziland and is bordered by Hlane and Mlawula. Mbuluzi has a marvellous diversity of habitat, from riverine forest to *Acacia nigrescens* savanna and open grassland. The reserve lists over 300 bird species and 100-150 birds can easily be recorded over a weekend visit. A bird hide is available overlooking the dam and the perennial Mbuluzi River winds through the reserve. The weather is hot and humid in summer but cooler in winter. The reserve offers fully equipped comfortable lodges and visitors have access to game viewing vehicles. There are maintained self-guided trails, giving visitors the opportunity to roam at will, or a guide can accompany you. Night drives are permitted for lodge residents. There is a campsite with ablution facilities overlooking the Mbuluzi River.

Ideal for viewing
- Narina trogon, African finfoot, crested guineafowl, eastern nicator, gorgeous bush-shrike, goliath heron, white-backed night-heron, great spotted cuckoo, crowned hornbill and woodland kingfisher.
- Impala, giraffe, hippopotamus, zebra, waterbuck, blue wildebeest, kudu, nyala.
- Foam nest tree frog, brown-backed tree frog, olive toad, flatbacked toad, painted reed frog.
- Leopard tortoise, Natal hinged tortoise, Wahlberg's velvet gecko, Moreau's tropical house gecko, southern tree agama, rock monitor, brown house snake, vine snake, Mozambique spitting cobra, puff adder, southern African python, Nile crocodile.
- *Albizia harveyi* (bushveld albizia)*, Pachypodium saundersii* (kudu lily), *Spirostachys africana* (tamboti) and a variety of aloes including *A. chabaudii* (Chabaud's aloe), *A. vanbalenii* (Van Balen's aloe), *A. rupestris* (Bottlebrush aloe) and *A. spicata* (Lebombo aloe).

MKHAYA GAME RESERVE

This private reserve is primarily a refuge for endangered mammals. Black and white rhinoceros, elephant, buffalo and a range of other species such as roan, sable and tsessebe are its main attractions, its birding potential is largely untapped. Mkhaya is mainly mixed *Acacia* woodland, but broadleaved woodland predominates in the north-western portion of the reserve. Examples of pristine riverine vegetation include some of the tallest *Breonadia salicina* (matumi) trees in the country. Over 7 500 hectares in extent, travel in the reserve is limited to guided game drives in open Landrovers and guided walks. However visitors may walk unescorted close to the comfortable overnight camp. The weather is hot and humid in summer but cooler in winter. This is a malarial area and the necessary precautions should be taken. You might reasonably expect to see around 80 bird species in a day during spring and early summer. The reserve is also home to Nguni cattle which were introduced to Swaziland over 1000 years ago.

Ideal for viewing
- African crowned eagle, black sparrowhawk, crested guineafowl, Verreaux's eagle-owl, African wood-owl, scaly-throated honeyguide, Retz's helmet-shrike, eastern nicator, bearded scrub-robin, pink-throated twinspot, green twinspot.

- Elephant, white rhinoceros, black rhinoceros, buffalo, roan and sable antelope.
- Guttural toad, olive toad, snoring puddle frog, foam nest tree frog, painted reed frog.
- Leopard tortoise, serrated hinged terrapin, Moreau's tropical house gecko, Wahlberg's velvet gecko, southern tree agama, Nile monitor, brown house snake, boomslang, Mozambique spitting cobra, southern African python.
- *Albizia anthelmintica* (worm-bark false-thorn), *Balanites maughamii* (greenthorn), *Erythrina humeana* (dwarf coral tree), *Boscia foetida* (bushveld shepherd's tree), *Bolusanthus speciosus* (tree wistaria), *Kigelia africana* (sausage tree) and *Breonadia salicina* (matumi).

MLAWULA NATURE RESERVE

This reserve is situated in north-eastern Swaziland, it has 16 500 hectares stretching from the lowveld plains to the top of the Lebombo Mountain range. The lowveld bushveld vegetation type covers most of the flat Siphiso Valley where game concentrates in high densities. The spectacular Lebombo Mountains rise out of the basalt plain and form the eastern boundary of the reserve. The mountain slopes are covered by broadleaved woodland, drainage lines support moist thickets and ironwood forests. On the flat-topped mountains, woodland gives way to open grassland and rocky outcrops. Mlawula boasts a bird list of over 350 species including a number of birds that are difficult to see elsewhere in the country. A list of over a 100 bird species is easily spotted in a day during spring and early summer. The summers are very hot, hiking is best in the cooler months, April to September. This is a malarial area and the necessary precautions should be taken. There are well graded roads for game driving and night driving is permitted. Fishing is permitted in the Mlawula River. Visitors have the choice of a stone cottage, self-catering furnished safari tents or camping.

Ideal for viewing
- White-backed vulture, thick-billed cuckoo, scaly-throated honeyguide, Retz's helmet-shrike,

MLAWULA RIVER

eastern nicator, purple-banded sunbird, bearded scrub-robin, African broadbill, African barred owl, grey sunbird and pink-throated twinspot.
• Waterbuck, kudu, bushbuck, nyala, zebra, hyaena.
• Longfin eel, lowveld largescale yellowfish, southern bulldog, leaden labeo, sharptooth catfish, Mozambique tilapia.
• Olive toad, flatbacked toad, red toad, snoring puddle frog, foam nest tree frog, brown-backed tree frog, bubbling kassina, green reed frog, painted reed frog.
• Leopard tortoise, Natal hinged tortoise, serrated hinged terrapin, Wahlberg's velvet gecko, southern tree agama, rainbow skink, Lebombo flat lizard, Nile monitor, brown house snake, yellow-bellied grass snake, boomslang, vine snake, puff adder, southern African python, Nile crocodile.
• *Encephalartos umbeluziensis, E. aplanatus,* the two endemics *Euphorbia keithii* (Swazi euphorbia) and *Aloe keithii, Ammocharis coranica* (ground lily), *Androstachys johnsonii* (ironwood), *Entandophragma caudatum* (wooden banana), *Ficus bubu* (Swazi fig) and the succulents *Gasteria batesiana* and *Haworthia limifolia.*

MLILWANE WILDLIFE SANCTUARY AND MANTENGA NATURE RESERVE

These two small reserves, making up 4 800 hectares, are situated between Mbabane and Manzini just off the touristed Ezulwini Valley. Mlilwane and Mantenga offer a surprising diversity for an area bedeviled with exotic vegetation in the form of guava, bugweed and gum, and carved with deep erosion furrows. The topography is undulating hills and flat plains, with the Nyonyane

MANTENGA FALLS

mountains in the north. The area is predominantly open grassland, but woodland extends along drainage lines and on the lower slopes of the mountains. Grasslands in the northern sections are fairly pristine with pockets of montane forest along drainage lines and ravines. There is an extensive network of good roads in the main portion of the reserves, while the northern portions are only accessible on foot. Guided walks, horse-riding, mountain biking and game drives are offered at Mlilwane where accommodation includes camp sites, safari tents, a rest camp and an upmarket lodge. This has a small botanical garden with interesting aloes and cycads. Mantenga has a beautiful waterfall, a cultural village with traditional dancing and accommodation in large furnished tents. Both reserves have restaurants.

Ideal for viewing
• African crowned eagle, black sparrowhawk, marsh owl, half-collared kingfisher, white-fronted bee-eater, buff-streaked chat, broad-tailed warbler, Cape grassbird, golden weaver, southern bald ibis.
• Zebra, blue wildebeest, hippopotamus, nyala.
• Guttural toad, red toad, common river frog, Natal sand frog, snoring puddle frog, painted reed frog.
• Giant Swazi flat gecko, Cape dwarf gecko, Wahlberg's velvet gecko, Moreau's tropical house gecko, southern tree agama, rainbow skink, Nile monitor, common brown water snake, common night adder, southern African python.
• The endemic *Senecio mlilwanensis*, the orchid *Polystachya zuluensis*, *Catha edulis* (bushman's tea), *Diospyros galpinii* (dwarf hairy jackalberry), *Heteropyxis canescens* (forest lavender tree), *Pterocarpus angolensis* (kiaat).

NISELA SAFARIS
Situated in the arid lowveld in south-eastern Swaziland this 1 500 hectare reserve has open con-servation areas as well as lion in large fenced pens and a mature crocodile in a pond next to the restaurant. There is a range of accommodation from camping to luxury rooms in a restored colo-nial farmhouse. Game viewing vehicles are available.

Ideal for viewing
• African fish-eagle, woolly-necked stork, Levaillant's cuckoo, acacia pied barbet.
• Lion, giraffe, waterbuck, kudu.
• Guttural toad, common river frog, snoring puddle frog, plain grass frog, green reed frog, water lily frog, painted reed frog.
• Leopard tortoise, Speke's hinged tortoise, serrated hinged terrapin, Cape dwarf gecko, Wahl-berg's velvet gecko, southern tree agama, common striped skink, variable skink, brown house snake, short-snouted grass snake, spotted bush snake, boomslang, vine snake, puff adder, south-ern African python, Nile crocodile.
• *Cordia monoica* (sandpaper saucer-berry), *Aloe parvibracteata, Acacia tortilis* (umbrella Thorn), *A. xanthophloea* (fever tree), *Balanites pedicellaris* (small green thorn), *Cadaba natalen-sis* (greenleaved wormbush), *Salvadora australis* (narrow-leaved mustard-tree).

WILD FLOWERS, MALOLOTJA NATURE RESERVE

PHOPHONYANE NATURE RESERVE

This 200 hectare reserve is in the north-west of the country and lies on the banks of the Phophon-yane River. There is extensive riverine bush and a series of attractive waterfalls and limpid pools. These are accessed from a network of walking trails which are ideal for viewing the prolific birdlife. There are chalets, furnished tents at the water's edge and a restaurant.

Ideal for viewing
• Pink-throated twinspot, green twinspot, black-bellied starling, narina trogon, African wood-owl.
• Red duiker, bushbuck, bushpig.
• Guttural toad, common river frog, sharp-nosed grass frog, snoring puddle frog, painted reed frog.
• Cape dwarf gecko, Wahlberg's velvet gecko, southern tree agama, rainbow skink, brown house snake, Natal green snake, spotted bush snake, vine snake, southern African python.
• *Sterculia murex (lowveld chestnut), Rauvolfia caffra* (quinine tree), *Cussonia natalensis* (rock cabbage tree), *Aloe spicata* (Lebombo aloe), *A. dyeri, Trichocladus ellipticus* (white witch-hazel), *Ekebergia capensis* (Cape ash).

SHEWULA NATURE RESERVE

Shewula is the only community based reserve in the country. Situated on the top of the Lebombo Mountains and covering an area of 2 650 hectares, it has spectacular views over the bushveld be-low. This is an opportunity to taste local food, sleep in a stone rondavel (thatched round hut) and pay a visit to the community traditional healer or '*sangoma*'. Hiking trails have been established to cater for all fitness levels.

Ideal for viewing
• African broadbill, dark-backed weaver, purple-banded sunbird, pink-throated twinspot.
• Samango monkey, red duiker, bushpig
• Guttural toad, olive toad, common river frog, foam nest tree frog, painted reed frog.
• Leopard tortoise, serrated hinged terrapin, Cape dwarf gecko, Wahlberg's velvet gecko, com-mon striped skink, rainbow skink, Lebombo flat lizard, Warren's girdled lizard, brown house snake, short-snouted grass snake, yellow-bellied grass snake, vine snake, southern African py-thon, Nile crocodile.
• *Boophane disticha* (fan leaved boophane), *Androstachys johnsonii* (ironwood), *Atalaya alata* (Lebombo krantz ash), *Lannea antiscorbutica* (pink-haired lannea), *Oeceoclades lonchophylla, O. mackenii* (orchids), *Uvaria lucida* (large-fruit cluster-pear), *Teclea gerrardii* (Zulu cherry-or-ange), *Ficus polita* (Heart-leaved fig).

COMMON ALIEN INVASIVE SPECIES

Flora

Chromolaena odorata
Triffid weed, Sandanezwe

Lantana camara
Common lantana, Bukhwebeletane

Solanum mauritianum
Bug weed, Isibongabonga

Acacia mearnsii
Black wattle, Umtfolo wesilungu

Psidium guajava
Guava, Emagwava

Fauna

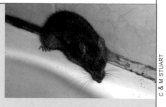

House rat
Rattus rattus
Ligundvwane

House
sparrow
*Passer
domesticus*
Jolwane

Common
myna
*Acridotheres
tristis*

Fish

Australian
redclaw
*Cherax
quadricarinatus*

Bass
*Micropterus
salmoides*

Trout
*Oncorhynchus
mykiss*

LINDA LOFFLER
BOB FORRESTER
KATE BRAUN
LINDA LOFFLER
KATE BRAUN

C & M STUART
NEIL GRAY
GINA JC WILGENBUS
ROGER BILLS, SAIAB
PAUL SKELTON
ROGER BILLS, SAIAB

GLOSSARY

Alien invasive – plant or animal introduced by man to a region where it does not belong. Because of the absence of natural competition and predators, populations may explode invasively.

Alpha male/female – the dominant male and female in group-living animals that do most or all of the breeding.

Antennae – paired sensory organs attached to the head of some myriapods, insects and crustaceans.

Anthers – the male, pollen-bearing organ in a flower, borne on a stalk-like filament.

Arboreal – living in trees.

Aril – a fleshy, coloured covering on a seed, evolved mainly to attract birds and insects which then distribute the seed.

Axil – the angle between a leaf surface and the stem which bears it.

Barbel – fleshy sensory appendage on the head, usually near the mouth, of a fish.

Beak – tortoise upper jaw (herpetological).

Biodiversity – biological diversity which refers to the total variety of life on earth.

Borrow pit – shallow gravel quarry next to roads rehabilitating naturally.

Bract – a small atypical or modified leaf situated at the base of a flower or on a stalk or pedicel.

Brood parasite – a bird species that lays its eggs in the nest of others with the result that the chicks are raised by foster parents, eg cuckoos, honeyguides and whydahs.

Browser – an animal that feeds on leaves, twigs or flowers.

Calyx – the outer whorl of a flower, made up of a number of sepals (calyx lobes) which protect the flower bud.

Carapace - upper portion of a tortoise or terrapin shell.

Caudal – of or like a tail.

Class – a large division of plants or animals that share certain characteristics, eg myriapods, crustaceans, insects, fish, amphibians, reptiles, birds, mammals.

Compound – made up of several similar parts, commonly applied to a leaf which is divided into leaflets; double compound: in a leaf, twice-divided or bipinnate.

Consumer – an organism that obtains its food by feeding off other organisms.

Coverts – non-flight feathers that line the wing both above and below.

Crest – prominent feathers that stick out from the top of the head.

Decurved - curved downwards.

Disc – digital pads (on toes).

Diurnal – active in the day.

Dominance hierarchy – order of dominance in group-living individuals.

Donga – ditch or dry riverbed.

Drupe – fleshy fruit surrounding a stone.

Echolocation – navigation by sonar where the animal emits a high pitched sound which bounces back off objects in its path and is then picked up through the ears. Micro-bats are best known for this.

Ecotone areas – transitional areas between vegetation types.

Elliptic – usually said of a leaf which tapers to both ends, and is widest about the middle.

Endemic – naturally found only in a particular and usually restricted geographic area or region.

Family – a group of related genera.

Foliolate – having leaflets, usually preceded by the number of leaflets, e.g. 3-foliolate or **trifoliate**.

Food chain – a list of organisms that shows the feeding relationship between them and the direction of energy flow.

Food web – a group of interlinking food chains that shows the feeding relationships between organisms.

Fossorial – living underground.

Fronds – the leaf of a fern, including the stalk or stipe.

Gall – an abnormal growth caused by infestation of a plant part by an insect or disease organism.

Gape – meeting point of upper and lower jaws.

Genus – a group of closely related species that share certain characteristics.

Grazer – an animal that feeds on grass.

Gregarious – animals which live in groups or communities.

Hibernation – dormancy in winter during which time animals typically drop their temperature to that of the surrounding environment.

Hinged terrapin – terrapin with a partially hinging plastron.

Hinged tortoise – tortoise with a partially hinging carapace.

Hybridization – cross-breeding between individuals that are genetically unlike such as different species or varieties.

Incisor – chisel-shaped tooth in front of mouth of mammals.

Indigenous – refers to organisms that are native to an area.

Inflorescence – a flowering shoot bearing more than one flower, arranged in various patterns.

Invertebrates – organisms that do not have a backbone.

Keeled – shaped like the keel of a boat.

Malar stripe – stripe on a bird's face from base of bill down sides of throat.

Mental lobe – a rounded extension protruding from the lower jaw on fish.

Moult – the replacement of worn feathers with new ones.

Morph – a permanent but alternative plumage colour.

Nape – the back of the neck of a bird.

Nocturnal – active at night.

Nuchal shield – small scale at the front of the carapace above the head on chelonians.

Obovate – of a leaf shape, roughly shaped like an inverted egg, widest in the upper half.

Order – a group of related families.

Organism – any living thing (e.g. bacteria, fungi, plants or animals).

Ovate – of a leaf shape which is roughly egg-shaped in outline, widest in the lower half.

Parasitise – see "Brood parasite".

Parotid glands – pair of raised, elongated glands behind the eyes of most species of toads.

Peduncle – the common stalk of a group of two to several flowers or inflorescence.

Perennial rivers– permanently flowing.

Petal – one lobe of the corolla, the showy and often colourful part of the flower.

Petiole – the stalk of a leaf.

Phalanx – bones of the finger or toes.

Pinnate – said of a leaf which is once-divided and having leaflets arranged in two ranks on opposite sides of the rachis.

Plastron – lower portion of a tortoise or ter-

rapin shell.

Plumage – refers to the entire set of feathers of a bird. Some birds, especially males, grow special brightly coloured breeding plumage during the mating season.

Prehensile – able to grip, usually in reference to the tail.

Primary consumer – first consumer in a food chain (e.g. herbivores).

Producers – organisms that make their own food using energy from sunlight through the process of photosynthesis (e.g. green plants).

Racemes – an inflorescence with a single unbranched axis bearing stalked flowers.

RDB - Swaziland Red Data Book, listing threatened species.

Riparian – on a river bank

Roost – refers to a particular site used for resting up by birds during the night or bats (and nocturnal owls) during the day.

Rufous – reddish.

Rupicolous – living on rocks (and in rock crevices).

Scrape – nest which is a simple scrape in the ground.

Secondary feathers (secondaries) – flight feathers that come off the fore-arm of a bird. Primaries are flight feathers that come off the hand of the bird; typically the longest feathers of the wing.

Sepal – a segment of the calyx; a calyx lobe.

Sexual dimorphism – condition in which the male and female of the same species are markedly different in size or colour.

Simple – of a leaf which is undivided or, if lobed, then less than half-way to the midrib.

Sorus (pl. sori) – the fertile body on a fern frond, composed of a number of spore-producing sporangia.

Species – a group of individuals that look alike, behave similarly and interbreed; different species do not (normally) interbreed in nature.

Spish/pish – a sound made by birders to draw a bird closer.

Spur – a hollow, tubelike extension of a petal or sepal.

Styles – in a flower the stalk bearing the stigma, borne on the ovary.

Swazi Nation Land – land held in trust for the nation by the King.

Tarsus – lowest bone in the leg of a bird,

below the ankle joint (or false knee).

Taxon (pl. taxa) – any unit of classification into which a living organism fits e.g. a family, genus, species, subspecies or variety.

Temperate – characterized by mild temperatures.

Tepal – a segment of a perianth (petals and sepals) which is not differentiated into a calyx and corolla.

Termitarium – structure built by termites in which they live. Termitaria often rise high off the ground to form familiar termite mounds.

Terrestrial – an organism that lives on land.

Territory – an area of habitat occupied by an individual (or group) which actively excludes intruders of the same species. Territories have the same function as hierarchies – to ensure that the fittest males breed and that mating can take place without interruption.

Tricuspid – three pointed beak.

Subtropical – characterized by warm temperatures.

Umbel – an inflorescence which has numerous stalked flowers arising from a single point; each flower may be similarly divided to form a compound umbel.

Ungulate – hoofed mammal.

Vertebrates – organisms that have a backbone.

HIKERS IN PINE VALLEY

BIBLIOGRAPHY AND FURTHER READING

Bills, R., Boycott, R., Fakudze, M., Khumalo, N., Msibi, J., Scott, L., Terry, S., & Tweddle, D. (2004). *Fish and Fisheries Survey of Swaziland (2002 – 2003)*. South African Institute for Aquatic Biodiversity, Grahamstown.

Boycott, R.C. (1992). *An annotated checklist of the amphibians and reptiles of Swaziland*. Conservation Trust of Swaziland, Mbabane.

Boycott, R.C. & Bourquin, O. (2000). *The Southern African Tortoise Book*. A guide to southern African tortoises, terrapins and turtles. O. Bourquin, Hilton.

Boycott, R. & Parker, V. (2003). *Birds of the Malolotja Nature Reserve, Swaziland*. Avian Demography Unit and Conservation Trust of Swaziland.

Carruthers, V. (ed.) (1982). *The Sandton Field Book*. A guide to the natural history of the northern Witwatersrand. The Sandton Nature Conservation Society, Rivonia.

Coates Palgrave, K. (2002). *Trees of Southern Africa*. New Edition. Revised by Meg Coates Palgrave. Struik, Cape Town.

Dlamini, T.S. & Dlamini, G.M. (2001). *Swaziland Red Data List*. In: Golding, J.S. (ed.): Southern African Red Data List. SABONET Report Series No. 14. National Botanical Institute, Pretoria.

Dobson, L. & Lotter, M. (2004). *Vegetation Map of Swaziland*. In: Mucina, L. and Rutherford, M.C. (eds.), Vegetation Map of South Africa, Lesotho and Swaziland: Shapefiles of basic mapping units. Beta version 4.0, February 2004, National Botanical Institute, Cape Town.

Hockey, P.A.R., Dean, W.R.J. & Ryan, P.G. (2005). *Roberts Birds of Southern Africa, VIIth Edition*. The Trustees of the John Voelcker Bird Book Fund, Cape Town.

Leeming, J. (2003). *Scorpions of Southern Africa*. Struik, Cape Town.

Leroy, A. & Leroy, J. (2000). *Spiderwatch in Southern Africa*. Struik, Cape Town.

Loffler, L. & Loffler, P. (2005). *Swaziland Tree Atlas – including selected shrubs and climbers*. Southern African Botanical Diversity Network Report No. 35. SABONET, Pretoria.

Marais, J. (2004). *A Complete Guide to the Snakes of Southern Africa*. Struik, Cape Town.

Monadjem, A. (1998). *The Mammals of Swaziland*. Conservation Trust of Swaziland & Big Game Parks, Mbabane.

Monadjem, A., Boycott, R.C., Parker, V. & Culverwell, J. (2003). *Threatened Vertebrates of Swaziland*. Swaziland Red Data Book: fishes, amphibians, reptiles, birds and mammals. Ministry of Tourism, Environment and Communication, Mbabane.

Mucina, L., Geldenhuys, C.J., von Maltitz, G., Lötter, M.C., Matthews, W., Rutherford, M.C., Dobson, L. & Powrie, L.W. (2005). *Afrotemperate, Subtropical and Azonal Forests*. In: Mucina, L. & Rutherford, M.C. (eds.), Vegetation of South Africa, Lesotho and Swaziland. South African National Biodiversity Institute, Kirstenbosch, South Africa.

Parker, V. (1994). *Swaziland Bird Atlas 1985-1991*. Websters, Mbabane.

Passmore, N.I. and Carruthers, V.C. (1995). *South African Frogs*. A complete guide. Southern Book Publishers and Witwatersrand University Press. Johannesburg.

Pooley, E. (1994). *The Complete Field Guide to Trees of Natal, Zululand and Transkei*. Natal Flora Publications Trust, Durban.

Pooley, E. (1998). *A Field Guide to Wild Flowers Kwazulu-Natal and the Eastern Region*. Natal Flora Publications Trust, Durban.

Schmidt, E., Lotter, M. & McCleland, W. (2002). *Trees and Shrubs of Mpumalanga and Kruger National Park*. Jacana, Johannesburg.

Sinclair, I., Hockey, P. & Tarboton, W. (2002). *Sasol Birds of Southern Africa, 3rd Edition*. Struik, Cape Town.

Skelton, P. (2001). *A Complete Guide to the Freshwater Fishes of Southern Africa*. Struik, Cape Town.

Skinner, J.D. & Chimimba, C.T. (2005). *The Mammals of the Southern African Subregion*. Cambridge University Press, Cambridge.

Stuart, C & Stuart, T. (1992). *Field Guide to the Mammals of Southern Africa*. Struik, Cape Town.

Taylor, P.J. (2000). Bats of Southern Africa. University of Natal Press, Pietermaritzburg.

Van Wyk, A. E. & Smith, G. F. (2001). *Regions of Floristic Endemism in Southern Africa*. Umdaus Press, Hatfield.

Van Wyk, B., & Malan S. (1997). *Field Guide to the Wild Flowers of the Highveld*. Second edition. Struik, Cape Town.

Van Wyk, B., & Van Wyk, P. (1997). *Field Guide of Trees of Southern Africa*. Struik, Cape Town.

THE TEAM

Richard Boycott (Fishes, Amphibians, Reptiles, Invertebrates) teaches science at Waterford Kamhlaba College. He has been involved in nature conservation for over thirty years in South Africa and Swaziland and was Warden of the Malolotja Nature Reserve. He co-authored the definitive work on Southern African tortoises, terrapins and turtles. He also co-authored the Swaziland Red Data Book on vertebrates and Birds of the Malolotja Nature Reserve. He authored or co-authored more than seventy publications on the amphibians, reptiles, fishes and birds of southern Africa. richjude@realnet.co.sz

Bob Forrester (Introduction and historical perspective, Geology and cross-sections) is a photographer and archaeologist. His photos appear in a wide variety of publications. He has written two books and edited several more. Recently he surveyed all rock art sites in the country, managed the opening of the Nsangwini Rock Art Site to the public and established the Interpretation Centre at Ngwenya, the world's oldest mine. He digitises old photos of Swaziland which are freely downloadable at www.sntc.org.sz/sdphotos/ bob@bobforrester.com

Linda Loffler (Vegetation types, Trees, Flowers, National parks and reserves, Common alien invasive species) is an environmental scientist and field botanist with extensive experience in consultancies and ecological assessments in Swaziland. She has been involved with biodiversity conservation in the country for many years, working with both private and government sectors. She has conducted research on Swaziland's flora for the past ten years and recently published the Swaziland Tree Atlas with Selected Shrubs and Climbers. *P O Box 764, Mbabane.* lindad@africaonline.co.sz

Prof. Ara Monadjem (Mammals, Birds) is an Associate Professor in the Biological Sciences Department, University of Swaziland. He has conducted research on Swaziland's birds and mammals, with particular emphasis on their ecology and conservation. He has written three books, numerous scientific articles as well as ecological assessments for various developmental projects and the Government of Swaziland. *Dept of Biological Sciences, University of Swaziland, Private Bag 4, Kwaluseni.* ara@uniswacc.uniswa.sz

Phil and Joanna Perry have produced and published several books on a range of wildlife related themes. Some of these have been translated into eight languages. Joanna laid out this book. Phil digitally processed all the photos. He is a noted wildlife photographer specialising in leopards. His wildlife photographs are marketed by Frank Lane Picture Agency and Images of Africa.

www.pperrywildlifephotos.org.sz

171

IMAGE CREDITS

SIBEBE ROCK

USEFUL CONTACTS

Places to visit
Big Game Parks (Hlane Royal National Park*, Mkhaya Game Reserve*, Mlilwane Wildlife
   Sanctuary*): www.biggameparks.org
Mbuluzi Game Reserve*: www.mbuluzigamereserve.co.sz
Mhlosinga Game Reserve (Ubombo Sugar Ltd): Dave Ducasse (+268) 624 9042
Muti Muti Nature Reserve: (+268) 437 1319
Ngwempisi Hiking Trail: (+268) 625 6004, e-mail: ngwempisi@mailfly.com
Nisela Safaris*: www.niselasafaris.co.za
Phophonyane Nature Reserve*: www.phophonyane.co.sz
Shewula Nature Reserve*: (+268) 605 1160
Swaziland National Herbarium: Malkerns Research Station, PO Box 4, Malkerns
Swaziland National Museum: (+268) 416 1179, www.sntc.org.sz
Swaziland National Trust Commission (Malolotja Nature Reserve*, Mlawula Nature Reserve*,
   Mantenga Nature Reserve*, Hawane Nature Reserve): www.sntc.org.sz

*Described in National Parks and Reserves, pp.158-165.

Organisations
African Bird Club: www.africanbirdclub.org
All Out Africa: www.all-out.org/countries/swaziland.aspx
BirdLife South Africa: www.birdlife.org.za
Lubombo Conservancy: www.ecs.co.sz/lc/index/htm
Natural History Society of Swaziland: www.naturalhistorysociety.org.sz
Yonge Nawe (Environmental Action Group): www.yongenawe.com

Government initiatives
Swaziland Tourism Authority: www.welcometoswaziland.com
Transfrontier Conservation Areas: www.sntc.org.sz/programs/tfcas.asp

Eco-tours
Swazi Trails: www.swazitrails.co.sz

SPECIES CHECKLISTS

Species checklists prepared by the Wild Swaziland team covering all species found in Swaziland can be downloaded free from the internet from these URLs:

- http://www.naturalhistorysociety.org.sz/Fauna_and_Flora.htm
  Checklists available:
  - Birds
  - Mammals
  - Reptiles
  - Amphibians
  - Freshwater fish

  Plus a list of siSwati names.

- http://www.sntc.org.sz/biodiversity/sdflora.asp — Flora
- http://www.sntc.org.sz/biodiversity/faunachecklist.asp — Fauna
- http://www.sntc.org.sz/alienplants/specieslist.asp — Alien plants

DRAINAGE LINE WITH TREE FERNS (*Cyathea dregei*) IN MONTANE GRASSLAND, MALOLOTJA

INDEX OF FEATURED SPECIES

HIPPOPOTAMUS